Stop People Pleasing!

How to Set Boundaries, Start Saying
No, and Take Control of Your Life

By: Derek Walker

Table of Contents

Introduction

It's a Friday afternoon. You're working late trying to catch up on your job because you agreed to help a coworker with a project. You're exhausted and you want to go home, but you can't because you are supposed to stop by a family member's house to let their dog out and water their plants. You have to cook dinner for your family this evening and wake up early tomorrow morning because your spouse wants help with a renovation this weekend. Your project is due Monday, and your kid is having a bake sale, which you signed up for because the teacher asked a few weeks ago.

Does this sound familiar? You're exhausted and you have a full agenda of plans ahead. You don't know when you're going to get some peace again, and there's no end in sight. Then someone comes up to you and asks for a favor. For some crazy reason, you say yes.

You may seem to have a problem saying no. It doesn't matter what you have going on. You see, there are people in the world who will mold themselves to be whoever they need to be in front of other people. These people, called people pleasers, can:

- *Find it difficult to say no because of feeling too worried or guilty about others' feelings and opinions.*
- *Say yes too quickly and find it hard to achieve everything they signed up for.*
- *Use small lies and excuses to get out of situations that they have overbooked.*

- *Commonly say sorry.*
- *Have a tough time accepting help and compliments.*
- *Rescue people often.*
- *Say yes because they're searching for validation and purpose.*
- *Commonly be exhausted and burnt out.*
- *Have trouble communicating what they actually need or want to be happy.*
- *Feel like their emotions and opinions don't matter.*

Some people will travel to the end of the world to make others happy. Some will swim oceans and walk miles to please those around them. While this may seem like a great quality to have, it can take a toll on people. When you're always being the giver, you might be a people pleaser. We run around trying to make everyone happy. We think we're okay and we will get a break once we are finished, but when you're a people pleaser, you never get a break.

Having all or some of the characteristics above can predict that you're a people pleaser. Being a people pleaser, or a giver, means you almost constantly have something going on. Whether you are swamped with volunteer committees at your kids' school or buried with projects at work, you are a busy person. If you're here, with me, reading this book, you know a few things:

1. You are wanting to learn more about what it means to be a people pleaser.
2. You're wanting to learn more about yourself.
3. You are wanting to make changes to your life, for the better.

People pleasers are also called givers because they give away parts of themselves to fit into communities and conversations. Givers will give their health, wealth, time, and resources in order to make others happy and comfortable.

You might be a people pleaser if you can't say no or keep making excuses for others. You are a people pleaser if others are consistently taking advantage of you. Here's a big one: you don't ask for help. No matter how overwhelmed you get, asking for help is your last option. Then when you do ask for help, you feel awful for asking. It's a lose-lose situation.

But let's not forget that we actually *do* want to help people. It can be our passion to help others with what they need. People pleasers can be a really great help for others. The problems arise when we are sacrificing too much of ourselves for others. These problems get worse when we lose ourselves trying to please others.

People pleasers are "givers" and those that are being helped are "takers." While givers are set in stone about giving (and takers are set in stone for taking), we need a little more balance. If people are constantly giving, there will be no one to take. Givers must get accustomed to taking occasionally. Even a flower must "take" from its environment in order to "give" pollen to bees.

People know that they can count on you when they need help. But these people are takers and they rarely set boundaries. It's important to understand when others are not setting boundaries when asking you for help.

As a people pleaser, it's important to take care of yourself. Being a "superhuman" may feel good but accepting everything asked of you can take a toll on your health—emotionally, physically, mentally, and spiritually.

When you're a people pleaser, you're stressed. You've taken on more than you can handle and you're looking for a way out. You tell yourself that next time you won't do it. But then the time comes and it's too hard to say no. That's what we are going to work on for the next ten chapters. We are going to discuss:

Chapter 1: Problems with Being a People Pleaser

In chapter one we discuss internal and external conflicts. Internal conflicts are struggles you have within yourself. External conflicts are issues from interactions with others and outside environments. During many times of conflict, it's easy to lose yourself. When we lose ourselves, we look to other people to boost our confidence. When we focus on the approval of others, we will do anything we need to do to be accepted. This leads to fake and faulty relationships.

Internal Conflicts
External Conflicts
Problems with Losing Yourself
Our Confidence Comes from Others
Fake and Faulty Relationships

Chapter 2: Discovering Who You Are

Chapter two is all about learning about yourself. We'll discuss personality tests that can be done to show you more about yourself. We also talk about creating a moral inventory to look at our most important priorities. Learning more about yourself can bring your attention to some unhealthy behaviors you have. These wrongful behaviors can result from poor self-confidence. Our poor self-confidence can be exacerbated by our inner critic. Our inner critic is the little voice in our heads that attacks us when we fail or make a mistake. We learn to avoid our inner critic and how to recognize when they are causing us damage. Chapter two finishes by discussing what our goals might be for reading the book.

> Learning About Yourself
> Unhealthy Behaviors
> Poor Self-Confidence
> The Loud, Loud Inner Critic
> Why Are You Here?

Chapter 3: The Psychology of People Pleasing

Our brains send out various chemicals and signals throughout the body. The chemicals are responsible for controlling many of our body's processes. Our past experiences and trauma can affect the chemicals and where they are sent throughout the body. When we have a lack of self-esteem, it can affect the amount of chemicals that are released in our brains. Being impressionable is also a sign of low self-esteem. Instead of focusing on low self-esteem, we can improve our self-identity and self-worth. We can improve these by understanding and altering our insecurities.

> Chemicals in the Brain
> Past Experiences and Trauma
> Lack of Self-Esteem
> Impressionable
> Self-Identity and Self-Worth
> Insecurities

Chapter 4: How to Set Boundaries

In chapter four, we discuss the various types of boundaries. Boundaries are important for protecting ourselves and others. We can use boundaries to keep ourselves from becoming too upset or exhausted to deal with other parts of our lives. Chapter four shows us how to create boundaries. Creating boundaries shows we have a compassion for ourselves. It can be hard to show yourself compassion and mercy, so some have trouble setting boundaries.

> Types of Boundaries
> How to Create Boundaries
> Self-Compassion
> Why Some Can't Set Boundaries

Chapter 5: How to Say No and Mean It

When you're a people pleaser, it can be hard (or even impossible) to say no. We may say yes, even when we know the answer is no, and cancel later just because we couldn't say no. This wastes our time and the time of others. We also must feel the pressure and anxiety related with cancelling plans. We learn more about saying yes out of desire, rather than obligation. Chapter five starts with tips for saying no to those who ask for too much, or when we've reached our limit. We can use positive language when saying no so it can "let them down easier." We learn that with saying no, there may be conflict. Chapter five discusses the potential opportunities that arise from conflict. Most importantly, standing out allows you to say no and mean it because you can boost your confidence.

Standing out makes you brave. You can say no and mean it when you're brave enough to do so.

> Tips for Saying No
> Difference Between Obligation and Desire
> Positive Language
> Opportunities of Conflict
> Standing Out

Chapter 6: Staying Strong

Chapter six starts with important coping mechanisms we can use to improve our anxiety and pressure we feel during tough situations. As a people pleaser, it can be easy to relapse into old ways while in a tough situation. It's important to stay strong during these interactions so you can create a long-lasting change in your life. Making a plan will improve your chances of leaving the interaction successful. Creating a team of support that you can fall on when you need them acts like a safety net. When you feel bad for saying no, or if you need a reminder why you're saying no, you can reach out to your support team for motivation. Your support team will also be able to help you handle reactions from others.

> Coping Mechanisms
> Make a Plan
> Support
> Handling Reactions

Chapter 7: Expressing Yourself

Expressing yourself means taking part in activities that make you feel happy and free. Expressing yourself can be done through various activities. These can range from being creative and expressing yourself through art, to driving a racecar at 100 mph. Everybody expresses themselves differently but being social is one of the great ways you can express yourself. You mingle and interact with others and show parts of yourself to new people. During self-expression, various parts of our brain are exercised. Over time, our brain can adapt to these changes and actually alter the way we think. Chapter seven ends with various ways that you can express yourself.

> Activities
> Social
> Brain Changes During Self-Expression
> Ways to Express Yourself

Chapter 8: Being Assertive

Being assertive means standing your ground. You're not being rude, but you're getting the point across. You can be polite but stern when telling people no. Chapter eight discusses the differences between passive, assertive, and aggressive. Being passive means you let anyone walk over you and take advantage of you (*coughs* a people pleaser). Being assertive is finding a middle ground between being a pushover and being rude. Being aggressive means being rude. You can be assertive when you give your message in a confident, clear, and controlled manner. Building a better mental health can help you when being assertive in tough situations.

Passive, Assertive, and Aggressive
Confident, Clear, and Controlled
Building a Better Mental Health

Chapter 9: What if Nothing is Working?

When you feel like you can't say no, or you are saying no but some people don't seem to be getting the picture, you feel like nothing you're doing is working. You may need help with time management. If you simply cannot start saying no, you can learn and use time management skills so you're not so tired and overworked. Some may need therapy to get through the reasons why they are a people pleaser. Having an outside voice gives us a better perspective of our life. We can use this perspective to pursue a thoughtful yes. You can say yes sometimes, but make sure it's a thoughtful yes. A thoughtful yes means you take the time to think about the request, and the outcomes, before saying yes. This gives you better chances of truly wanting to do the request.

Time Management
Therapy
A Thoughtful Yes

Chapter 10: Make a Game Plan

When you want to start change within, you need to make a game plan to take it with you. Once you decide to implement change, you're taking steps to a happier life. Chapter ten goes over various things you can do every day to give yourself a happier life. Something as simple as changing your mindset can change your entire outlook on life. Chapter ten also breaks down what therapy is and how it can be beneficial for everyone. You'll also be able to find some in-depth descriptions of some common mental health disorders that people across the world experience.

Implementing Change Within
Steps to a Happier Life
Therapy

The book will walk you through some thoughts and behaviors that you didn't know you had. Throughout your reading you are going to relate well with parts of the book and be able to connect your life scenarios with information you come across. The goal of the book is to teach you what you need to stop being a people pleaser in the short term, and act as a form of motivation in the long term.

After reading you'll be able to:

- *Better control your responses when being asked something.*
- *Say no and stand behind your answer.*
- *Cultivate the self-confidence and independence to set boundaries and stick with them.*
- *Learn more about yourself.*

This book can act as a great future reference when you need to refresh your skills or regain your motivation. You can save the book and return to it when you need it again. So, let's get started!

Chapter 1: Problems with Being a People Pleaser

Life is hard enough as it is without us adding more problems to our plate. When it comes to real life, a situation is based on the outcome rather than the intention. You may have good intentions, but if you end up messing it up, then you must deal with the consequences. The good intentions can't cover the damage done.

So, even though you may be doing something from the heart, it can still end up backfiring on you and others. While your heart is in the right place, you must make sure you have the resources (time and energy) to follow through. Otherwise, it could lead to unfortunate and uncomfortable outcomes.

Being a people pleaser can be dangerous. It can lead to quite a few problems in your life. Constantly aiming to please others is a servant lifestyle. While this is helpful for those who are in need, it can be rough on you. You cannot continue helping and taking care of others if you don't take care of yourself.

Being a people pleaser creates both internal and external conflicts. An internal conflict is a battle on the inside. It's like the devil on one shoulder and an angel on the other. When you're having an internal conflict, you're battling some rough emotions and feelings. This hurts your mental, physical, and emotional health.

When you're battling someone or something else, then you are having an external conflict. External conflicts involve an opposite party and external forces. No matter whether a problem is internal or external, it's something that stands in the way of reaching our goals.

Internal Conflicts

So, what happens during an internal conflict? For one, you are arguing with yourself. You aren't sure which decision to make. Being a people pleaser can cause many internal conflicts by making you sometimes choose between yourself and others. You sacrifice your thoughts and goals in order to accommodate someone else's needs.

You may not notice the internal problems that being a people pleaser brings. People pleasers tend to take part in self-sabotaging behavior in order to improve the outcomes for others. You may not understand the damage being done, because you're too busy trying to solve your internal struggle.

When you're a people pleaser you have to adapt to social situations. You aim to mold and shift parts of yourself so you can fit in, in all situations. One party trick for you: you can become a chameleon.

People pleasers constantly search for external validation. These givers put high stakes on an external person making decisions about their self-esteem and their self-worth. This type of validation can only be healthy if it is found within.

Being a people pleaser also causes harm to physical, emotional, and mental health. Focusing on what others think about you can distract you from your personal health symptoms. Sometimes when you're helping others, you can be blinded by the happiness of others.

Some of the personal problems that come with being a people pleaser include:

- _Sadness:_ When you're constantly focusing on how you can help others, you lose sight of what makes you happy. You are more likely to prioritize others' needs before your own. You can't be happy when you're not working toward what makes you happy.

- _Sacrifice:_ You are sacrificing your time, work, health, and more when you agree to help others. You sacrifice your needs.
    - When we sacrifice our happiness, values, and time for others, we are depending on them for our outcomes. When we devote ourselves to someone else, we have someone to blame if we fail or if something goes wrong.
        - This can be a hard pill to swallow. You may think, "I couldn't get this done because of someone else." In reality, if you had told the person "no" initially, you wouldn't be in the situation you were in.

- _Lying:_ When you automatically say yes without thinking, you have to come up with an excuse or a lie to get out of it because you're either exhausted or you've overbooked yourself.
    - You also lie to yourself and others when you say, "I'm tired" and "I'm fine" when we both know you're not. You lie to others when you tell them you don't mind the extra work, but in reality, you're dreading it.

- _Loneliness:_ When you are constantly having to adapt or lie to those around you, rather than being yourself, it can seem lonely. You may act a certain way or say certain things that you wouldn't when you were with others. You get lonely when you feel like no one knows the real you.

- _Exhaustion:_ When you're trying to prioritize too many things at once, you'll tire yourself out trying to get it all done. Your mind and body will fight for both goals even if they are in opposite directions. Exhaustion may creep up on you and lead to problems with thinking, driving, paying attention, extreme mood changes, appetite changes, and more.

- _Disappointment:_ Not only do you get disappointed in yourself for failing to help others sometimes, but you also get disappointed with others for not being as appreciative as you need.

- _Guilt:_ When you finally have to say no, or if you fail trying to help someone, you feel guilty. You'll feel guilty even if you tried as hard as you could.

- _Difficulty Expressing Feelings:_ As a people pleaser, it is against your nature to express unhappiness about something. Complaining or confessing when your feelings are hurt is not something you are used to. This means you grow further away from those you love and care about.
    - You are more likely to avoid conflict to keep those around you comfortable. In order to avoid conflict, you have to stifle your

emotions. This decreases mental health. Plus, you're less likely to stand up for those you believe in.

- *Self-Worth Dependence on Others: When we are a people pleaser, we live on the approval of others. We want them to say thank you and realize the hell we just put ourselves through for helping them. When they don't express as much gratitude as we need, we can start to doubt our self-worth.*

- *Negative Thoughts: Most of the time, people pleasers are self-critical. They focus on their actions and what they don't get done. They don't live their success long enough because they are moving on to the next way to say yes.*

Internal struggles can be lonely. They can cause damage to our health. It's best to remember to cut ourselves some slack so we don't get caught up in self-discipline. But we will talk more about that in the later chapters.

External Conflicts

As if internal struggles aren't enough, being a people pleaser can also lead to problems in our environment. This means our friends, family, work, and more are all affected by our people-pleasing actions. While you want to help as much as possible, it's easy to slip over that line from helping to hurting.

When you can recognize problems that are arising from people-pleasing, it's easier to see the effect it's having on you. Let's talk about some of the external conflicts you experience when people-pleasing takes over.

- *Fake Relationships:* Fake relationships come from the front you use when trying to adapt to social situations. When you change who you are in front of certain people, it makes them view you a certain way that others won't. This creates a conflicting view of you from various people, eventually confusing you on who you really are.
  - When people only see certain versions of you, or the versions you want them to see, they will not know you. They will not know how to love you. This degrades trust and respect.
  - When you need people you've worked so hard to help, they may not be there for you.

- *Resentment:* When you are unable to express your true feelings, you begin to resent those around you. When you begin getting upset with how you're being used and treated, but you don't talk with them, you start to resent them for putting you through too much. This can greatly damage those relationships around you.

- *Manipulation:* When people understand that you are reliable, dependable, and helpful, they will want to ask you for more. People can take advantage of your helpfulness and use it to advance their goals.
  - Oftentimes a boss will ask a loyal, hardworking employee (a.k.a. you) for a favor because they know you will say yes. When the boss is consistently asking for your

help, and no one else's, this can be a sign you are being manipulated and being taken advantage of. It can also grow resentment for your boss and your job.

- *Decrease in Performance: When you are overwhelmed, you are not operating at your best level. This means that your life and work performance will take a nosedive. While you may think you're being productive, sometimes you're just running really fast in the same spot.*
  - *When you say yes to someone, but you don't mean it, there is a higher chance you won't perform as well as if you wanted to do the job. You could waste your time and theirs.*

- *Goal Sabotage: When you're trying to help others, you temporarily put your goals on hold. You tell yourself, "I'll hold off until I can just finish this for another person." You make plans to get back on track. Then you end up helping someone else until you're to the point that you forget you even had a goal.*

- *No Passion: When you are constantly sabotaging your goals and focusing on others, you lose sight of yourself and your life. When you have no passion, you feel like you have no purpose. Our passion is what keeps our eyes on the prize. Now we don't even know what we want anymore.*

Do you know how important it is to find a passion? A passion is what gets you up in the morning. It brings you so much happiness. It is what you work toward in life. Your motivation. The funny thing about passion is everyone has one, they just have to figure it out. Or you know what your passion is, and you've just lost sight of it.

When you help others, you are helping them achieve their passion. While this is a really great thing, it can damage your future if all you can do is help other people. You may feel you are no longer your own person but an extension of the needs of others.

Problems with Losing Yourself

When you're always focused on others, you lose who you are and who you're supposed to be. From the second we are born we go through changes and new experiences. These little moments, every day, add up to who we are today. These small decisions and choices and interactions change us each day. Sometimes we may notice it while other times we cannot.

Over time, we create this personality. We find out things that we love about ourselves and things that we hate about ourselves. Throughout our life, we learn to put parts of ourselves in a box to adapt to other situations. After a while, though, that box can disappear. And it can be hard to find it.

When we don't know who we are, it's hard to know what we want. When we don't know what we want, we don't know what to do. We can feel lost in this black hole, moving through life in routines. Our lives were built for so much more than just routines. Routines can be hard to break, but they're worth it in the end.

When you've lost yourself, it's harder to build relationships. You don't know what you want in people. You don't know what you like and don't like in people. But, once you learn more about yourself, you can understand what you want and deserve in relationships.

Our Confidence Comes from Others

We aim to please. We go out of our way to help people. We live on the approval and acceptance of others. We will mold and bend ourselves to fit various situations like clay. This holds us back. When we're worried about what others will think, we can't focus on what *we* think. Our words and actions become built upon those of others, rather than our personal beliefs and behaviors.

Being a people pleaser can become a norm. When something is a norm, it's normal to you. You may not even realize you're doing it. So, when we don't get a strong enough "thank you" or adequate praise for our actions, we start to be self-critical.

Could I have done that better? Was it something I did wrong? Are they upset with me? These questions all run through our minds. It is hard to fight off these negative thoughts when you're stuck in the routine of pleasing others. Your mind is focused elsewhere. You think you have other needs you attend to. You think you're strong enough to handle it. Sometimes, we're wrong.

When we are more confident, we express ourselves better. We believe that we will fit into any social situation with our *own* special interests. When you're molding into a conversation, you are just speaking to them. But, when you add your own thoughts and feelings, you can see the passion behind your words. That's what makes you a great person to be around and to talk with.

When we don't have to focus on the praise of others, we can spend more time praising ourselves. Now, we know that sounds so easy to say. "Just be nicer to yourself" or "just say no." Yeah, it sounds easy. There's actually a lot of processing that goes into being nice to yourself and saying no. But that doesn't mean it's not doable. It just takes time and practice.

People pleasing has been said to be a way of emotional dependance on others. It gives us an excuse to disregard responsibility for our actions because we were helping someone else. People pleasing can be an emotional crutch.

People pleasing is a way of avoiding discomfort and displeasure from others. It is a way of shifting the responsibility for our happiness onto others. When you give so much and get nothing in return, you start to question your self-worth and your relationships. Meanwhile, it has nothing to do with the fact you are receiving nothing back; it has everything to do with the reality that you give too much. Therefore, they are taking too much.

Plus, saying yes to a favor you don't actually want to do means you won't have true meaning and purpose when helping them out. It could waste both your time. You could both find another person to work with that would be a better match. If you say yes then fail at their task, you'll feel like you've lost, *and* they won't have any help. It's a lose-lose situation.

Fake and Faulty Relationships

As a people pleaser, it's hard to trust many of our relationships. People can befriend a people pleaser for the wrong reasons, and we think we're being helpful. Takers can take advantage of givers and only be their friend to benefit from them. Givers can be naturally compassionate, so they may not know when they're being taken advantage of.

When you are a people pleaser you feel obligated to give 150% to every relationship you create. This can be with friends, coworkers, family, and more. You will plan every minute of your day in regard to others and their schedules. Unfortunately, your group can take advantage of this.

They will know that you are the one who normally reaches out to make plans. You do this to put effort into the friendship. You want to be a good friend and aim to make others happy, so you set up lunches and movie dates.

Then, these people can get used to you being the one to reach out and set up plans. They won't reach out because they know you will. They won't make plans or make an effort because they know you will. Even in the real relationships, people can leverage your kindness.

When friends and family ask you for something, knowing you won't say no, it's taking advantage of you. If a friend knows you're really busy but they want you to help them move, they can ask you because you won't say no. They use their selfish agenda to overwork you because you are willing to let them.

Bosses may ask you to do all of the extra work because they know you will. They know you're underpaid and overworked, but they still need that project done, so they ask you. They don't ask any other employees because they might say no. They ask you because it's almost a guaranteed yes.

When you help others, you are "spoiling" them. You are showing them that you are dependable and capable of helping them when they need it. You're able to be there for support and you don't complain when doing so. So, they ask you a second time. And a third. Then a fourth. But when you ask for something in return or express a different idea, they completely shut you down because they're not used to you speaking out.

Some of these relationships would disappear if you were to say no or stop people pleasing. One of the toughest situations people pleasers can be in is if they truly care for another person but all that person wants to do is take and not give.

To understand if a relationship is toxic, think back to the times you have helped them out. Were they appreciative? Did they say thank you? Did they return the favor? Do they always ask for something when you're not around? Do they offend you? Think on your answers and determine if it's a real or superficial relationship.

Some people don't like the behavior of people pleasers. Some people see it as weak, having no backbone, annoying, and fake. If you are acting one way in front of certain people, then another way with others, people can see you as fake. They may think that you're changing your personality to fit with others, which is what you're doing. Although you don't have intentions of misleading or offending others, you may still end up doing that if your people-pleasing behaviors are more unhealthy than healthy.

When you feel like you're not getting the recognition you deserve, you start to feel resentment for those you're helping. While they think you're just being nice and helpful, they're actually taking advantage of you. Since most people pleasers don't want to have a conflict, they won't say anything. This unspoken animosity will ruin the friendship or lead to a blow-up fight.

Living with this resentment for others is not healthy for you or them. You may be passive-aggressive without knowing it. You may make demeaning comments unconsciously or say something "jokingly" (even though it's not really a joke) which can lead to conflict.

You may also be addicted to their love and attention. If you feel like you need ultimate acceptance from those around you, then you could tire yourself out trying to gain their approval. Their tasks and requests make you feel special because you are getting attention. If people are willing to do that to you, then they may not be worth having in your life. So, you go through all of this trouble just for them to snub you or reply with more tasks and questions.

When you're so involved in what others think, it can affect your self-identity. If you're trying so hard to fit in when you don't, you may tell yourself that you think certain things or act certain ways. You don't really feel or act like that, so you end up confused on who you are and who you are telling yourself to be. When you don't know who you are, you can't build strong, authentic, genuine relationships.

To overcome problems, you must find out more about yourself. When you know who you are, you know how to get out of problems, and you trust yourself to do so. In the next chapter, we will talk more about how to discover who you truly are and how to build your self-confidence.

Chapter 2: Discovering Who You Are

Who am I? We've all heard the dreaded question: tell me about yourself. It's as though the question shuts our brain down and we can't think of anything we've learned about ourselves. It can be harder to think when you're put on the spot, too. But stop and think about it. Do you really *know* yourself? Or do you just know *about* yourself?

When you know yourself, you understand yourself. You can feel your emotions and understand where they're coming from. You are better able to adapt your feelings to comfort yourself and stand strong in your thoughts. Knowing yourself means knowing how you will react in certain situations. It means being able to explain your actions and emotions to others, as well as yourself.

Knowing about ourselves means that we know things on our surface. You like certain foods. You like to do certain things. You could tell people some of your favorites and some of your dislikes. You can talk about your experiences and things you have yet to experience.

For example, let's say you love to plan all of the big events in your life (wedding, birthday, etc.). Now, in your head you are doing everyone a favor by bringing people together and having a celebration. Your friends and family want to help you with the celebration, so they decide to decorate the back yard. You are furious they didn't check with you first. But, knowing yourself means you know *why* you are doing what you're doing.

When you know *about* yourself, you know you're angry because they went behind your back. You truly felt like you were no longer in control of the entire party and that scared you a little, so you lashed out with anger. When you know yourself, you know why you do what you do. This way, you don't place blame on others, and you are better able to calm yourself down.

So, knowing yourself well is a critical part of relationships. As you've seen with the decorating, you could avoid an argument if you realize why you're angry and understand that it's okay. We can't rely on other people to make ourselves feel better.

Learning About Yourself

There are tons of ways to learn more about yourself.

1. *Start a journal. You can do this a few different ways. You can jot down your random thoughts every night before bed. It can be what you did that day, what you plan to do tomorrow, what you liked, what you didn't like from your day, etc. Or you can get writing prompts online. These can come in the form of questions or generalized statements.*
   a. *For example: If you won $10,000 on a lottery ticket, what would you spend most of your money on? What would you buy first? Who would you tell first? Why?*
   b. *These prompts allow for people to be creative with their writing, in a guided way. That way, the creativity can flow without you having the pressure of thinking of something. You'll surprise yourself with what you learn.*

2. *Make a list of what you like and don't like.* This list
   can be broad or simple. You can make a lot or just
   one. You will think of things you enjoy that you may
   not have realized bring you joy before.
   a. Some lists to start with are favorite foods,
      least to favorite holidays, favorite to least
      movies, TV shows you don't like, etc.

3. *Create a moral inventory.* This is a great way to find
   out what matters to you the most. You will see what
   you value the most in your life and it will show you
   your passion.
   a. Create a list of everything that matters to
      you. It can be work, family, being a good
      spouse, friends, animals, being successful,
      helping homeless people, being a kind
      person, etc. What are some things that
      matter the most to you? Now cut that list in
      half. If you wrote down 20 things, find the 10
      that you think are the most important in that
      list of 20. Then, find the 5 most important
      things, to you, on your list of 10.
   b. You will get down to your top three
      priorities. These are your motivations to
      keep going. These are what you value most
      in life. This will guide your direction the rest
      of your life.
   - This is a great exercise to repeat throughout your
     life. As we grow and change, so do our priorities and
     values. It will also remind you of the "why" of doing
     what you do.

4. *Take a personality test.* There are various online
   personality tests that you can take to reveal more

about your personality. Your personality is what makes up who you are. These tests can tell you whether you're more of an extrovert or an introvert. Or if you're more open or closed.

    a. One of the better online personality tests is The Big Five (or Five Factor). The Big Five breaks down the human personality into five categories: openness, conscientiousness, extraversion, agreeableness, and neuroticism. The Big Five focuses on traits instead of types of personality.

    b. The Jung personality test tells you about yourself and how you relate to others. It compares your answers with various Jung types and shows you more about yourself and how you fit into certain careers.

5. <u>*Learn from experience.*</u> *You can also learn who you are through your experiences. Think of a time you were in a rough situation. Think of the toughest situation you have ever gone through.*

    a. What did you do during the situation?
    b. What did you do to make the situation better?
    c. Were you happy with the way you reacted?
    d. What would you have changed?
    e. What did you learn?

Once you answer these questions, focus on those answers. You will be able to see what you learned from every experience you endured. Did you expect yourself to be as strong as you were? Remember the feeling you have now. The pride you are feeling for making it through that tough situation.

It's in these tough situations that we learn the most about ourselves. This is because we normally go with a gut instinct: fight or flight. This is our go-to response to stress and threat. When we are under pressure, we find out what we can handle. After all, diamonds are formed from coal under pressure.

Now, think of a time when you have agreed to help someone, but you fail. Let's say your child has a play, a friend asks you out for a drink, and your neighbor needs you to let their dog out. You don't want to cancel and upset your daughter and friend, so you say yes to them. You know you really don't have time to help your neighbor, but you *want* to, so you say you'll make time.

You end up forgetting the dog while in a rush to your child's play, so he messed on the carpet. Now you and your neighbor are both upset and it's because you felt obligated to help. If you had said no then you would have felt guilty, but your neighbor would've found someone else who had the time to get it done.

When we fail to be everything we want to be, it can hurt our feelings. It's not a fun experience being in this mindset. So, we all understand what it's like. However, this feeling is the sign of growth.

Growth isn't comfortable, but it's necessary. This feeling shows us what we don't want to do in the future. We can learn from this and recognize the growth that this tough situation has given us.

Unhealthy Behaviors

Habits can be hard to break. Bad habits can especially be hard to break. Bad habits that we've had for a long time, even a lifetime, may feel like they will never change. Sometimes, even if it's a healthy behavior, it feels alien to us. We are so used to these unhealthy behaviors that when we experience the healthy way, we don't know how to react.

Learning more about ourselves allows us to start learning why we feel the need to be a people pleaser. You can learn more about your behaviors and actions that are unhealthy due to being a people pleaser. Once you recognize these unhealthy behaviors, you'll be able to change them for the better. Some unhealthy behaviors to look for in your everyday activities are:

- *You have more of an emotional investment in others than you do yourself.*
- *You feel responsible for other people's happiness.*
- *You avoid saying no.*
- *You try to balance multiple things at once, even when stressed out.*
- *You give an immediate answer (yes!).*
- *You overthink and overanalyze everything.*

When you are emotionally invested in others, you get too mentally exhausted trying to also care for yourself. You tend to sacrifice time from yourself to help others. This means you are investing your time and energy in places other than yourself.

You may feel responsible for the happiness of the people around you. There can be many reasons for this. Maybe you make the most money in your family. Maybe you are the oldest sibling. Maybe you are the most successful. Regardless, it's important to learn that the burden is not solely on you. People are also accountable for their own happiness.

You avoid saying no because you may be afraid of the outcomes. "They won't be my friend anymore," or "What will they think if I don't help?" The fallout is almost never as bad as we think it will be. It's best to be honest now rather than dishonest in the future.

You feel like a superhuman who can help anyone, just because you want to. You say yes to all aspects of your life. You are being pulled in 100 different directions. You may think you're helping, but you could be taking time away from your true friends and family.

If you're not good under pressure, then you sometimes automatically say "yes" because that's what you feel like you should say in that moment. That's because "yes" can make a situation go away or a conversation end when you're dealing with a taker. You don't necessarily think about it. You just know that you are committing yourself to someone else.

People pleasers may overthink and overanalyze because they are perfectionists. They want all things perfect and to meet their expectations. When something doesn't go the way people pleasers had planned it, they could dwell on it for days.

You can spot unhealthy behaviors when you notice them interfering with your life. If you can truly handle 4 – 5 tasks at a time, then there's no question you're an avid multitasker. However, there are probably times when you feel like you're going to explode. That's when you know that you're starting to cross boundaries.

Some signs that you are approaching unhealthy behavior include:

- *Trouble sleeping/eating*
- *Loss of appetite/motivation*
- *Panic attacks*
- *Anxiety*

- *Obsessive thoughts or actions*
- *Depression*
- *Quick weight gain or loss*
- *Frequent mood changes or laughing/crying episodes*

Normally at the point we start to feel uncomfortable is when we start to realize our boundaries. Sometimes we choose to pass those boundaries, thinking we can handle it. This is where the unhealthy behaviors start to take over.

Think of a time when you were super stressed out about work. What were you doing differently that made you so stressed at the time? Were you doing multiple projects or tasks at once? Did you accept more work to please others? Even if you successfully finished the work, it was torture working through. Was it worth the sleepless nights and frequent panic attacks? Sometimes we are so busy with our eyes on the prize that we don't see what's happening right in front of us.

That's why it's so important for us to know and understand ourselves. What makes us tick. When we better understand ourselves, we better manage ourselves. When we can better manage ourselves, we can affect the people around us more positively. The best way we can help others is by being honest. That first step to being honest is being honest with yourself.

Poor Self-Confidence

One of the biggest reasons to learn about yourself is to improve your self-confidence. So, what makes up self-confidence? Self-confidence is your thoughts on your ability to handle a certain situation. Self-confidence is a lot more important than what you may think.

When you think of a long and happy life, what do you think about? Family and work goals? Trips? Regardless of what the rest of your life has planned, self-confidence is associated with every part of a fulfilling and happy life.

When you have strong self-confidence, you have less anxiety and fear. When we get overwhelmed and stressed, our negative thoughts fight their way in to tell us, "I can't do it." When we feel confident, we can quiet this voice and tell ourselves, "I can do it."

When we aren't very self-confident, we mull over previous mistakes and decisions. We constantly think about what we did wrong and what we could've done differently. Instead of this being a negative situation, you can focus on what you learned throughout your mistakes. This way, you can be sure they won't happen again. You can't change the past, but you can learn from it.

Having unbreakable self-confidence will lead to greater motivation. You can look back to previous rough times. Think about how you were able to make it through that situation. When you're confident in your abilities to do something, you can use your past times of success to motivate you to make it through.

Not only can being a people pleaser affect relationships, so can self-confidence. As contradictory as it sounds, the more self-confident we are, the less we focus on ourselves. Have you ever walked in a room and thought, "They all think I look weird" or "Everyone is staring and picking me apart"? I'm sure we all have. In reality, though, other people are more worried about themselves than they are you. You are your biggest critic, so you assume everyone else feels the same way.

When you're self-confident you stop worrying about what others think of you. You stop thinking of your every move. Now you can actually interact with other people and have a genuine conversation. You'll have a better time during your conversation because you won't be so worried about the impression you're making. You also won't be making comparisons between yourself and others. Not to mention that when you are relaxed in the conversation, those around you will relax and it will lead to a better interaction.

If you have low confidence, then you need more help when it comes to obstacles and failure. You're not able to use the coping skills that come with confidence. Now, self-confidence doesn't mean you'll never fail. It means that you'll be able to better handle it when you do fail. Your resilience will come from confidence in yourself to do even better the next time.

Without confidence you can't love and understand yourself. When you are confident you have a better idea of who you actually are. You have more of a sense of yourself. You can understand that your weaknesses don't define you and they don't affect your self-worth.

If you've got self-confidence you may be lucky. There are people all over the world that don't have any confidence. But you can learn to improve your confidence. When you feel confident, you feel like a rock star. You feel like you own every room you walk into. Yes, that sounds egotistical. But sometimes we have to hype ourselves up, because there may be no one else who can do it.

The Loud, Loud Inner Critic

You know that little voice inside your head that shouts things at you when you fail at something? Yep, that's our inner critic. Our inner critic is such a hateful thing, and if we let it take over it could ruin parts of our life. The inner critic reads the present, predicts the future, and idolizes the past. The inner critic is constantly pulling up past events and situations and using them as an "I told you so" argument. They attempt to convince you things will go wrong.

Being a people pleaser means that you listen to the inner voice that makes you feel bad if you say no to something. It makes you scared of what will happen when you say no. It convinces you that the world will just practically fall apart if you tell someone you can't help them.

Our inner critic (critical inner voice) scolds us when we feel like we need it. When we fail or do something wrong, your inner critic takes that as a one-way ticket to critique. This critic can be really judgmental and harsh. It brings shame and depression. So, an inner critic can make or break your mental health, potentially making it harder to interact with others and yourself.

This inner critic makes you feel pressure to say yes, even when you don't think you can handle it. But then when you take it and fail, your inner critic attacks you for it. There's no winning! That's one of the biggest reasons why being a people pleaser over-activates our inner critic (or our inner judge).

The problem with the inner critic is that it can seriously cause you some mental harm. Imagine if that demeaning voice inside you was a person on the outside of you saying the same things. It sounds awful, doesn't it? Why do we do that to ourselves? People are all wired differently. Some don't think twice about giving, while some won't think twice about taking. When these people meet it can lead to an unhealthy relationship.

Our inner critic isn't all that bad. It can support us when we win and praise us when we are successful. We get extra pride from hearing that praise from the inside. We become really proud of ourselves. Which is proof that just as harmful as the inner critic can be, it can also be helpful. We don't want to get rid of the inner critic completely; we just want to train them on what to say and when to say it.

Why Are You Here?

Why did you pick this book today? What were you thinking when you decided to read? Do you want to get something from it? Do you want to see if you relate? Are you curious about seeing what a people pleaser is?

You can find out what you're made of by setting goals for yourself. Goals are important for giving you motivation and purpose. But you have to make sure you're setting appropriate goals for yourself. You can't set a huge goal and expect to reach it, then get upset with yourself if you don't. It's a completely unhealthy situation that can actually hold you back from accomplishing real goals.

You can set S.M.A.R.T. goals for yourself. S.M.A.R.T. goals are:

S – Specific: When you're setting goals that are too broad, you have no way of tracking your progress. Therefore, you won't know if you're actually being successful. Having a specific endpoint to the goals means you have something to work toward.

M – Measurable: You need to be able to track your progress; that way you can see when you're going to meet a goal, whether it be big or small. It's important to be able to see when you're going to make an achievement because it acts as motivation to finish out strong.

A – Attainable: Make sure that you can actually accomplish the goal. For example, saying, "I am going to lose twenty pounds in a week" is setting yourself up for failure. There's a thin line between confidence and cockiness. Setting attainable goals keeps you challenged and motivated to reach the goal.

R – Relevant: Your goal should benefit you or your beliefs. If you plan to raise money for charity, you will gain the happy feeling that comes with helping others. If you make goals without your personal emotions, you're going to have a harder time reaching those goals.

T – Time-Bound: Set a timeframe. This keeps you focusing on the endgame. If you just set a goal but no timeframe, you won't feel any pressure to get it done. A little pressure is good because it can keep us going. When you have an endpoint, you are more motivated to take steps to success.

An example of a S.M.A.R.T. goal is wanting to read five self-help books in thirty days. This is a S.M.A.R.T. goal because it's specific. You describe the action you want to do and the type of book you want to read. It's measurable because you're going to be able to see your progress. After you've read three books, you'll see you only have two left until meeting the goal. It's attainable because you're able to pick any self-help books, big or small. You can decide how fast, or slow, to read. The goal is relevant because it is going to positively affect you directly. Last, it's time-bound because you have an expiration date on the goal.

Chapter 3: The Psychology of People Pleasing

We are standing there having a conversation. The person we are talking to is talking about how busy they are. They are discussing their work, their social life, and their home life. We can feel our heart rate pick up because we know they're about to ask us for a favor. More than likely we've been dreading this interaction because we knew it was going to lead to being asked for a favor. They ask you the favor and you immediately say yes. You don't give yourself time to think. You don't give yourself time to object. You just say yes.

There are also the people who jump at the opportunity to please and help others. It's those parents who volunteer for everything at their kids' school. It's the ambitious coworker who wants to impress the boss. It's the cousin who won't express their political views at Thanksgiving due to upsetting the family. Now these aren't bad things. But if we do them constantly, they lead to bad outcomes.

Parents can get so overwhelmed volunteering at their kids' school that they lose sleep, their work performance takes a dive, and even relationships crumble and fall apart. The coworker was so involved with impressing their boss that they upset other employees and now they are in trouble with Human Resources. The cousin that won't speak up about their political views will feel isolated and alone even in a room full of family members.

Millions of years ago, cavemen would gather in groups to improve chances of survival. It allowed protection and sharing of the work required to live. It pooled resources and allowed socialization between group members. In this case, if you weren't accepted as a part of the group then you would probably die. Now, it may feel like that today. But it's almost never as serious as we think it is.

It's innate that we feel we have to fit into the group, as people pleasers. It's also innate for us to be social to be healthy. Being social has many positive benefits on mental health and can prevent some conditions like anxiety and depression. It is in our nature to be involved with other people. Little to no contact with the world can lead to some different behaviors than normal.

People-pleasing is a habit, a knee-jerk reaction, and an automatic yes for some people. They don't think twice about it and are happy to help any and everywhere they can. How are these people different from others? How are they okay with always giving?

People pleasers get exhausted and frustrated with themselves. They get angry with themselves for making plans or overbooking themselves to keep everyone happy. We wonder, "Why did I say yes? I'm not doing this again," but let's be honest, it's going to happen again.

When we get in these situations where it happens again, why do we feel the need to say yes? There is some ominous black cloud hanging behind our backs waiting to explode when we say no. We feel pressured to do everything we can and be everything for everyone. Why do we feel like this?

Why do I feel the urge to please? You get the urge and motivation to people please from various places.

Chemicals in the Brain

Our brain controls everything we do, from forming a sentence to digesting food. Our brain plays a critical part in every bodily process. It only makes sense that the brain can control our people-pleasing urges. Where do they come from in the brain?

When we touch someone, get close to them, or interact with them positively, our brain releases the neurotransmitter oxytocin. Oxytocin is associated with trust, empathy, relationship-building, and sexual activity. When you are trying to get close with others, your brain releases more oxytocin.

Our brain likes oxytocin. It's associated with positive interactions and can improve mood. Because our brain likes it, it craves more. That's why our body wants to keep people-pleasing. This is because our brain wants more of the oxytocin that's produced from helping others, especially if helping others makes you happy.

We all know and love serotonin. It's important for regulating mood and making us happy. Serotonin is also associated with various processes in the brain and is secreted in parts of the brain from interactions with others. Serotonin is responsible for affecting eating, digestion, sleep, mood, learning, cognition, and more.

When we interact with others, laugh, and smile, our brain secretes serotonin which makes us happy. Just like with oxytocin, the brain likes serotonin and will want to do more things that give serotonin.

Dopamine is another neurotransmitter in the brain that deals with the way we feel pleasure. Dopamine is important for motivation, learning, sleep, mood, attention, and pain processing. Too much dopamine in parts of the brain can lead to delusions and hallucinations. Too little in other parts can lead to lack of desire and motivation.

If we lack oxytocin, serotonin, or dopamine, we may lack the motivation and desire to work on our own goals. We may focus on others and help them with what they need as a distraction for not working on our goals.

If we have too much oxytocin, serotonin, or dopamine, we may be over-motivated to help others with things they need. We may be manic, having a high episode of energy and signing ourselves up for one hundred things. When we crash, and we always do, we regret taking on so much.

Past Experiences and Trauma

Things that we have gone through in the past are a part of our character and personality today. If we knew then what we know now, we wouldn't be who we are. Past trauma has an influence on our decisions and comes consistently into our head. Some people have gone through things in their life that have forced them to become people pleasers. They may not even know there's a name for it. They just know they can't say no.

Children who feel like they must compete for attention from their parents may turn into people pleasers. When parents aren't tuned in to their children's lives, it can create a void in the child. The child then does whatever they need to do to get their attention. People pleasers can begin as parent pleasers.

Parents' emotional inconsistency is one of the biggest predictors for becoming a people pleaser. The child feels as though they have to be the caregiver of their parents because their parents can be wrapped up in their own lives. This creates the fantasy that the parent should be protected, and the child must grow up quickly to be emotionally responsible.

At this point, the child feels they must earn their parent's love. Because of this, they adapt to a people-pleasing lifestyle so they will consistently be popular and loved. They feel the need to make others happy so that they can be happy. This can be considered a form of emotional abuse.

This is considered emotional abuse because the children begin to blame themselves for anything going on in the parent's life. They aim to act completely good and not rock the boat and upset anyone further. When in reality, the parent is more worried about their life than they are their child's.

During any form of trauma, whether it be short-term or long-term, it can affect the chemicals in our brain. It can cause new connections to be made and can erase old connections. For example, if you got bit by a snake at a local lake, every time you think of that lake you are going to think of your snake bite.

These changes in our brain can lead to changes in our behavior. While it may seem normal to us, we can be engaging in people-pleasing behaviors unconsciously. Because of the trauma, it's harder to notice.

In the event of abuse, it can make someone a people pleaser. After long periods of abuse, some may feel that they must follow the rules and stay in line to be safe and loved. This can take a while to change and may even become a lifetime problem if they never bring attention to it.

Once we have been through trauma, our brain attempts to make sure we are safe and that it won't happen again. Our brain will do things to try and protect us, such as creating alternative personalities and blocking out certain times and experiences.

People may fold into being a giver after trauma because they feel like their thoughts and opinions don't matter. They've been groomed to think that they are unwanted, and that they don't matter. They will be terrified of saying no. People pleasers think it'll be easier to go along with what everyone else thinks, instead of fighting for themselves.

People pleasers who came from trauma feel guilty when they get angry. This is because they have probably experienced gaslighting in the past. Gaslighting happens when someone makes you question your memories, thoughts, sanity, and beliefs. When you get angry now you may brush it off as nothing because "you are overreacting."

People pleasers can have a defensive mindset. People pleasers set out to help others because we think they're going to hurt us, and we are constantly aiming to protect ourselves. Simply put—we don't want to experience bad feelings.

When we people-please we are avoiding conflict. This is a safety measure people pleasers take from their past trauma and use to protect themselves. When you agree with someone, there shouldn't be reason for conflict.

Lack of Self-Esteem

Self-esteem is the confidence someone has in their own abilities and self-worth. When you're a people pleaser, you are more focused on the feelings and emotions of others, rather than yourself. Low self-esteem leads to fear of failure or rejection. We fear being wrong, so we agree with others. Even if we think there is something else that can be said or done, we go along with what others think.

If something fails, we can blame it on the task, rather than accept responsibility. We're afraid of rejection so we aim to fit in with others. We will do what it takes for others so we can feel included in the group.

When others don't agree with our thoughts, we tend to think those thoughts are invalid. Since people pleasers need validation, if they don't have strong self-esteem then they can be crushed by others' comments and denial.

A lack of self-esteem can lead to people-pleasing behaviors. This is because we need a constant boost from others. We look for that through doing favors and making plans and promises. We try to use others to make ourselves feel better.

Some may see people pleasers as being emotionally selfish. It is said that people pleasers are only being nice to get the validation and affirmation that we crave. It's ironic, don't you think, that a people pleaser can be seen as selfish? It can be hard for a people pleaser to be selfish. We so rarely think of our well-being that we take the opportunity to be selfish.

While people pleasers are using others for love and approval, what they're seeking isn't necessarily a bad thing. That's why it's not exactly considered "selfish." These positive desires can eventually, however, put a damper on our lives.

Those with dark desires can take advantage of the people pleasers. We are a target for those who want to exploit others because they know we will say yes. Being a people pleaser means being put in various situations where you are stuck between a rock and a hard place.

People pleasers aim to feel good about themselves from the approval of others. This turns to co-dependency. This means that you have a large amount of emotional reliance on another person. Their actions determine your reactions, which can lead to a very risky relationship.

With low self-esteem comes low self-validation. Low self-validation means you have a high reliance on others and how they determine and affect your thoughts and beliefs. If they think your ideas are silly, so will you. If they think your beliefs are shallow, so will you. When we have low self-esteem, we have high rates of external validation.

People pleasers have problems with self-love. They question their worthiness of appreciation, value, and adoration. Even when they crave validation, they may get uncomfortable with all the attention and try to shift it onto someone else.

Impressionable

People pleasers may want something in return, even if they don't *know* they want something in return. Some people are nice because they expect others to be nice to them. They expect a positive outcome from their positive actions.

Or someone may be very nice to a boss to get themselves noticed or get a promotion. Some people pleasers may accept questions and opportunities for selfish reasons. This could be to improve themselves or their job performance. However, some people are just impressionable.

When you are impressionable, you are easily influenced by your outside environment. New trends, styles, and other people can make us mold ourselves without noticing. Some people pleasers find new things interesting and simply want to take part in the new event.

These people may not necessarily be pleasing people on purpose, but simply being influenced by them. They are not wanting or avoiding something; they are simply trying to learn about new parts in their surroundings.

When you're impressionable, you may start using mannerisms and terms you may not have used before. You may change your clothes or studies to follow a new trend or concept. Some people realize they are impressionable, and others don't. It's easier for people pleasers to be too impressionable and lead to unhealthy, people-pleasing behaviors. Not only are we molded by other views, but we are also focused on our views' effects on those around us.

People pleasers can obsess over their impression on others. Because they have such a strong fear of rejection, they will pick apart their actions with a magnifying glass. Our inner critic will be having a field day with every mistake we make. Givers want to give as much comfort to those around us as possible. The more we can fit in, the more comfort we can give.

Not only impressionable, people pleasers are also emotionally intelligent. People pleasers are so impressionable because of their emotional intelligence. They can read behaviors, feelings, and social cues in the situation to be able to alter themselves to fit in. If they're not able to read the situation correctly, then they won't know the things to say or do to fit in.

We may embarrass ourselves to relieve any tension in the room. We may crack a joke when the mood is low, or everyone seems tired and sad. Our times to try and help can be shot down, though, which will negatively affect us.

People pleasers can feed off other people and their energy. Since they are emotionally co-dependent on others, it's easy for them to feel the same as those who are surrounding them. If you have all hateful and angry coworkers, chances are that as a people pleaser, you are also hateful and angry after being around them.

If people around you are happy and cheery, even if you're not, you're going to act happy and cheery. You can tell the people around you are comfortable when they're smiling, moving around, touching each other, and standing or sitting in a relaxed manner. If those around us are happy, then we are happy.

Because givers are impressionable, they are compassionate. They feel strong sympathy for others and try to please when people are uncomfortable or upset. They may also be naturally compassionate.

So, people pleasers can be completely compassionate or in the game for different reasons (expecting something in return). The biggest difference is that someone who is genuinely compassionate will still take themselves into account. Compassionate people see themselves and others as equals, with no one being more important than the other.

Many people may not know they're impressionable. Sometimes they are considered curious. Curious in the sense that when people pleasers experience something new they want to try it. Sometimes they can over-commit. They can feel inspired and motivated to take steps toward their newest obsession because they are so sure that it's what they want. It may only be what they want because of who they're around or what they're doing in their life.

It's important for people to know when they are impressionable because they can recognize this inspiration and motivation from something new, instead of experiencing an epiphany that they've just found their passion. At this point people can pursue this new path, while losing sight of their own path. And when they get so far down that path, it's hard to get back. Impressionable people can stick to their own path while still veering off occasionally for new experiences. They understand that this is temporary, and they have their own path in life.

Self-Identity and Self-Worth

People pleasers can pride themselves in helping others. Unfortunately for people pleasers, this means depending on others to determine our self-worth. People pleasers surround themselves with people who they think they deserve to be around. If they have little self-worth, they're likely to hang out with meaner people because they think that's what they deserve.

We may have low self-worth for many of the same reasons we are people pleasers: low self-esteem, impressionable, low confidence, etc. If we don't think much of ourselves, how can we expect other people to think and act any differently?

When people pleasers do things for others, they feel worthy. They find their self-worth through being able to help others. We are only as good as much as we can help. Our self-identity is based on how much and how well we can help and please others.

Some people pleasers identify as people pleasers. They know that's what they do and think that's who they have to be, just because that's how they are. They feel trapped by the obligations of being a people pleaser. From this pressure, they act out of feelings of obligation.

When people pleasers are not needed, their self-worth can plummet. Because givers are so invested in other people's thoughts of them, when they don't have the opportunity to help others, their self-worth can't improve. When people pleasers aren't needed, their entire purpose for living may feel like it's crashing down.

It's dangerous to be emotionally dependent on others because if you have no one, then self-worth plummets. If you lose the ability to help others, you could fall into a depression with a poor quality of life.

People pleasers get pleasure from helping others and being successful in pleasing others. If you don't have much self-worth, then it's easy to get a positive feeling from helping others. You may think that you don't matter, so any sacrifice you have to make is worth it if it means you can help someone else.

Nobody can determine your self-worth or your self-identity except you. You control that about yourself. You treat yourself the way you think you should be treated. You can do simple things such as telling yourself nice things to improve your self-worth. It doesn't matter what other people say or do. Your self-worth is for you to control.

Insecurities

Insecurities are uncertainties about yourself. You lack confidence in certain areas, and it makes you anxious. You have certain traits that you don't like about yourself and will go out of your way to make sure they aren't discovered.

People pleasers can have many insecurities that motivate them. Insecurities are common in people pleasers because they are constantly searching for validation from others. If they think they don't look good in an outfit, they will ask others for their opinion. If they are insecure about their appearance, they won't contribute their answers in a meeting.

It is said that people pleasers can lack the internal compass that allows us to understand the value of our actions. We don't know actually how "good" our actions are, so we need reassurance from others. When we don't think we know how good our actions are, we lack the confidence to believe ourselves.

This also makes it harder for us to determine when enough is enough. We want to believe the best in people because we believe the worst in ourselves. We're unsure about our abilities to say no or speak up, so we stay quiet to people please.

When you're insecure you can get jealous. Jealousy can lead to people-pleasing behaviors to gain someone's attention. You may agree to have dinner with a friend because you know your ex-partner will be in the same restaurant. You tell your neighbor you will let their dog out so you can use their big television. When jealousy is the motivation for being a people pleaser, the outcomes are usually selfish.

Parents can make children insecure from simply telling them what to do without letting them express themselves. The parents reward the children with love and affection when they obey, rather than act out of their own thoughts and behaviors. This teaches children they must obey, rather than think for themselves, to fit in.

This results in a pattern in the child to think they must please to be loved. This is especially true for women who are groomed at a very young age to be accommodating to others.

Everyone has insecurities. You may look at supermodels and think that they feel the best about themselves. You may look at people on the street and think, "Wow, I bet they have it all figured out." This isn't true. While you are jealous of someone else for being skinny, someone may be jealous of you because of your gorgeous hair. A guy driving a minivan may be jealous of a guy driving a Ferrari. Meanwhile there is someone on a bike jealous of the guy in the minivan because he has a car. Then there is someone at the bus stop who is jealous of the bike rider because he has a bike. Last, there is a crippled man in a wheelchair on his balcony, who is jealous of the man standing at the bus station.

The grass isn't always greener on the other side. Your insecurities can also be controlled by you. It can be hard to change, but you control whether something about your body bothers you or not. You may not be able to physically change it, but you can mentally change it. You can change your perception of your insecurities so that you see them as opportunities for improvement instead of problems.

Chapter 4: How to Set Boundaries

Think of an ex-partner who really broke your heart. I'm sure some of us, for a while, put up walls so no one could get in and hurt us again. Then when we meet someone, after some time, we decide to let down our walls. These emotional walls you have set up for yourself are boundaries.

Boundaries are like invisible bubbles. They are around you and with you at all times, but only you can see them. Safety and sanity come with boundaries. They allow you to comfortably stress yourself to see your limits but keep you from crossing boundaries. When you have strong boundaries, it shows those around you that they cannot cross them.

Boundaries are there to protect you, as well as others. It keeps you safe from overexertion when you obey them. It's important for you to set boundaries to keep your relationships in check. They are used to show where someone should stop before upsetting you or themselves. It is a type of warning that if someone crosses that boundary there will be consequences.

When you have boundaries, you have space to be yourself and show integrity. People will not respect your boundaries when they don't understand the difference between you and your boundaries. For example, think of someone crowding your personal space. While this may be a boundary for you, they are simply wanting to get closer with you or seeing how far they can push you before you bring it up.

These people think they're entitled to their thoughts and feelings without taking yours into account. That's why it's important for us to be able to stand in our confidence and respect ourselves.

Boundaries are important for any healthy relationship because they allow you to gain trust from others. With the constant overstepping of boundaries, it can make it harder to trust other people.

Even with boundaries, though, people pleasers may abandon them when they need them the most. They fear conflict and losing a relationship. A people pleaser will break their own boundary if that means saving the relationship.

People pleasers may also choose to break their boundaries because they feel guilty for saying no or upsetting someone else. It doesn't matter how much it limits or damages them, as long as they can save distress from another person.

Types of Boundaries

Boundaries can be set by us for any and all parts of our lives. They are our decision, and we can choose when or if we want to use them. Boundaries can be set for your sexuality, personal space, possessions or stuff, thoughts or emotions, energy and time, ethics, culture, religious views, and so much more.

There are various types of boundaries that exist and can be crossed: ethical, psychological, emotional, verbal, and physical.

- *Ethical boundaries go against our beliefs of right and wrong. Think back to the moral inventory we created in chapter two. Imagine if someone were to go against any of your top three priorities. This would be an ethical boundary.*

- *Psychological and emotional boundaries affect yourself and self-esteem. People can break psychological and emotional boundaries by judging, lying, criticizing, and demeaning. Gaslighting can also be a form of breaking boundaries. People can break these boundaries by using information you told them in confidence against you.*

- *When people are breaking these boundaries, they are making fun of you, your thoughts and emotions. They aim to shame, embarrass, and bully you. These people will try to make people pleasers feel guilty and responsible for others and their situations.*

- *Verbal violations of boundaries include preventing you to speak and talking over you. It can be interrupting you. Verbal violations also include gossiping about you and defaming your character.*

- *Crossing physical boundaries, as you can assume, means someone else putting their hands on you without your permission. This includes getting into your personal space or even using your belongings without asking. Physical violations also involve violating privacy and being inappropriate.*

There are times when employees must turn into people pleasers for their boss. They are made to say and do things to keep their job or earn an upcoming promotion. The boss expects these employees to make this sacrifice for the organization, regardless of their beliefs.

Many bosses believe that their thoughts and beliefs are more important than those of their counterparts or staff. Because managers tend to have more power than employees, it can be easier for them to get others to do things they normally wouldn't want to do. Setting boundaries can help protect you from this.

Some of the benefits of setting boundaries are having better self-esteem, more independence, and conserving emotional energy. When you set boundaries, you are making yourself a priority. You are drawing a clear line between yourself and other people.

One of the great things about boundaries is that they are flexible. They can change with you. When you're not willing to occasionally bend on certain boundaries, it can create problems with relationships. If you're not willing to let someone know more about you, you can't expect them to stay and love the real you.

It's important to understand the flexibility of boundaries. However, if you're continuously bending the boundary then you need to reassess your plan. Women are more prone to setting bendy boundaries because they feel the need to accommodate others.

When you have boundaries, you can save your emotional energy. If you let people walk all over you, you will come to resent them because you can't set boundaries. Setting limits can prevent you from getting angry with others.

Boundaries can also be different for each person, setting, location, comfort level, and more. The flexibility allows us to create boundaries in various situations. This gives us the ability to take a step back and understand our thoughts and what might happen next, if a boundary is crossed.

Having this emotional space gives us room to be vulnerable and grow. We can observe the environment and assess our boundaries after interacting. When we do this, we can have an easier transition between emotions.

You define your own boundaries. It's a personal choice and is different for everyone. We shape boundaries based on a number of things. Boundaries are shaped by culture, heritage, religion, social patterns, family dynamics, and life experience.

We all come from different families and pasts. We all have our own boundaries and ways of engaging with them. We can alter our boundaries as we grow and mature. Our perspectives can move with us as we learn and have new experiences. Everyone is different, but we must all be comfortable with ourselves to be able to deal with ever-changing boundaries.

When you're defining your boundaries, it's important to understand what your rights are. Your rights are basic interactions between yourself and others. For example, you have the right to make your needs as important as the needs of others. You have the right to be treated with respect. You have the right to accept failures and mistakes. We may feel like we have to be so hard on ourselves, because it's hard to remember that we *do* have these rights. We just have to remind ourselves.

When you find and believe in your rights, it'll be easier for you to stand by them. This way, you stop pleasing and pacifying others who don't honor your rights. This saves us from emotional drainage.

When you think someone may be breaking your boundaries then listen to your gut. When you start to feel discomfort or anger then they are likely passing a boundary. You may also find out that you need to set up a new boundary.

Your body will give signs on whether or not you can handle the situation (heart rate, sweat, tight throat, stomach, chest, etc.). You could clench your teeth when someone stands too close to you or get an increased heart rate when someone in the family mentions your dating life.

Focus on how others are treating your boundaries. Remember back to our list of top three values? Reflect on the feelings you have in situations where those boundaries have been challenged. Maybe someone threatened your family member and family is one of your most important values. The way you feel when those boundaries are pressed will mimic the way you feel if another boundary is being challenged.

How to Create Boundaries

Creating boundaries is up to you. You decide when, how many, why, where, etc. Boundaries are a way you can take control of your life. Creating boundaries should be personalized to you and what you want to achieve in life. You determine a level of self-respect when you set boundaries and you are investing in your health.

When you are creating boundaries, look at the ones you have now. Take note of how you created them and the limits surrounding the boundary. Look at the places where you don't seem to have any boundaries. Why is that? You can assess your life and determine where you need new boundaries.

You can set boundaries if you have recently experienced something you don't want to again, or if you want to stop some things that are already happening. You can create boundaries in a few ways.

1. *Be assertive.* *Know that what you say stands, regardless of what they say or do. If we back down from our boundary once, they will push the rest of them.*

2. _Learn how, and when, to say no_. It's important to understand that you can say no.
3. _Keep your spaces safe_. Don't rush yourself through feelings or criticize yourself during reflection. You don't need to yell at yourself while you're trying to figure it out.
4. _Get a support system._ You need people in your life who are going to be able to give you confidence and keep you reliable to staying strong in your "no."
5. _Reflect and learn._ Once you put the boundary in motion, make note of the first few interactions with it. If you like the outcome, keep the boundary in place until you think it's necessary to change it.

Think of a recent time when you've been really hurt or upset. Did you tell yourself "never again"? Did you swear off whatever it was that caused you pain? That's a boundary we can set up for ourselves out of anger. We decide we won't do something anymore because of emotions we are feeling at that time.

Now, some of us are stubborn and decide to stick with the boundary, regardless of the situation, because of such terrible emotional trauma. When you set boundaries while in an emotional state, they could be unrealistic or too strict. Then when you decide to break that boundary, you may blame yourself or others for the negative consequences. You can set immediate boundaries in tough situations but it's important to reassess these boundaries when you're calmer.

If something makes you uncomfortable, you don't have to take others into account when making boundaries. Women may avoid speaking out on sexual harassment in the workplace due to fear of repercussions. Although her boundaries may be crossed, she feels like she can't hold them in place without affecting her career and colleagues.

To create boundaries, you have to be in tune with your emotions. You have to understand what makes you happy and what makes you upset. When you pay attention to your emotions, you will know when you need to create a boundary.

When you keep your spaces safe, you feel more secure. You feel more secure because you know there is less of a chance of something getting hurt or ruined. Your spaces are not only mental but also physical. You can protect things that mean a lot to you and keep safe information about yourself.

Keeping your space safe means you know you want to keep it private. It is a thought or emotion that you don't want anyone to know. It is saving your energy for another situation. There are parts of us that have to be kept safe, or it will affect our health and quality of life.

You can keep your spaces safe in a variety of ways:

- *Use a locked drawer or safe box to hold private items.*
- *Use a digital journal with a password instead of a paper journal.*
- *Don't respond to business emails and texts sent to personal emails and phones.*
- *Set a time that you will stop accepting work or business calls.*
- *Use PINs, codes, and passwords on devices.*
- *Make use of the Do Not Disturb and silent features on devices.*
- *Make sure to schedule time off at work in advance.*

- *When you're on vacation, send an "out of office" reply.*
- *Turn off notifications for messaging or work apps while you're not at work.*
- *Schedule yourself some alone time to do anything you want.*

There are new studies that prove taking time out of our day for ourselves is good for physical and mental health, work performance, quality of life, and much more. Being in constant communication with your work may make you feel pressured to be available when needed. This can cause problems in life and in relationships.

Getting support is one of the best things you can do to improve your motivation and confidence in your boundaries. Support can come from many areas including:

- *Family*
- *Friends*
- *Coworkers*
- *Bosses*
- *Mentors*
- *Teachers*
- *Counselors*
- *Therapists*

You can get support for your boundaries whether they be physical or mental. When you are having trouble creating or sticking to a boundary, you can reach out to people on your support team for advice and help.

Your support team is helpful for reminding you why you set the boundary. They can use your past and examples to walk you through the situation with and without boundaries. They can motivate you to carry through with your boundary even when you are in a rough position.

Self-Compassion

Setting boundaries is a great way to practice self-care and compassion. You respect yourself enough to create lines that people shouldn't cross. Being self-kind means comforting and soothing yourself when you're in trouble or suffering.

Healthy boundaries promote good mental and emotional health, have a positive influence on others' behaviors, help in avoiding burnout, improve creating your identity, and increase developing autonomy. Healthy boundaries are critical for self-care.

When you have healthy boundaries, you can have less stress and find more fulfillment in your professional life. This leaves more room for your personal life. If you don't set healthy boundaries, you're prone to wasted time, financial burdens, stress, and more.

When you accept it, having compassion for others can be the same as compassion for ourselves. We have compassion when we see others hurting. We must have compassion when we see ourselves suffering.

We have to learn to set some boundaries with the inner critic. Think about if someone else was in your shoes. For example, if you don't get a promotion at work, your inner critic starts to attack you for what you could've done better. We need to say, "I worked hard for this. It's going to be okay." Have compassion for yourself when you're upset.

When you have compassion for someone, you forgive them for mistakes and understand that conflict is a part of human life. You can have this compassion for yourself when you make a mistake as well. Tell yourself what you would tell a friend who is going through the exact situation you are.

Automatically brushing off our difficult times can bottle up our pain. Ignoring our emotions can keep them bottled up inside until they explode. Don't brush them away, but instead welcome them in. Focus on the emotions in that time. Understand them, comfort and care for yourself, and be patient during this time. Don't try to rush your emotions to get through it faster. Let them take their own time. This gives you better chances of preventing those emotions from popping up in the future.

When you understand that bad things happen to everyone, and we all live with an open heart for reality, you are showing compassion for yourself and others. We are all human. We can all have compassion.

When you have self-compassion, you are capable of handling critiques and mistakes. To increase self-compassion, understand you are going to make mistakes. An entire part of a person's life is making mistakes. Whether you know it now or later, everyone makes mistakes. Instead of being so rough with yourself, understand this is a part of life that everyone has to go through.

Even if we want to set boundaries, sometimes we just can't. We may be able to set boundaries in some areas, but not all of them. There are some situations where it's really hard for us to set boundaries. Our actions are determined by whether or not we can stand by these boundaries.

Why Some Can't Set Boundaries

Some people can set strong boundaries and never fault on them. Some don't have concrete boundaries and live life creating them at the times they need them. Some don't know how to set boundaries. Others just don't know how to function with them.

Boundaries can limit what we want but protect what we need. Humans are reluctant to set boundaries because it takes things away from them. If they need to set boundaries but can't, there might be a problem with abuse or addiction.

A lack of self-esteem can be a sign of a lack of boundaries. Some aren't comfortable enough to stand their ground when someone is pushing against a boundary or causing discomfort.

The approval of those around them is important to people pleasers. People pleasers can want people to approve of them immediately and in all circumstances, so they will do what they can to gain that approval. That includes bending and breaking boundaries.

The lack of boundaries can be a sign of fear. Fear of standing up for oneself or drawing lines can prevent the set-up of boundaries. People who fear boundaries may not have learned how to separate their needs from others. They see the needs as situational. In some circumstances, needs change and that requires change on the people pleaser's end.

Fear of the fallout from expressing the boundary keeps many away from creating boundaries. When boundaries are disrespected and broken, people can become confused, outraged, scared, defensive, and aggravated.

Being stubborn also prevents boundaries from being successful. When we can't listen to ourselves to focus on the boundary, we may lose our sight and forget we placed the boundary. When you set a boundary, you are aiming to honor your own limits. If you don't honor your own boundaries, how can you expect others to do the same?

When you don't have boundaries then you're almost positively going to reach a breaking point. When you reach this point you may yell, panic, and cut someone off completely. Our survival instinct kicks in and we will end the relationship because it's doing us too much harm.

Now, these people are probably angrier with themselves for not setting boundaries instead of the other person, they just may not know it. At this point it would be misplaced anger. It is an inner conflict that turns into an external conflict.

Setting boundaries is hard. You must determine what you like and don't like, when to use them, when to move them, how to interact with them, etc. It's harder for people to set boundaries when they have mental illness.

Mental illness causes many, many problems with creating boundaries and keeping them intact. Boundaries require mental energy, as well as healthy mental conditions. Your brain doesn't have enough energy to constantly fight between mental illness and boundaries and everyday life at the same time, all of the time. It can also be harder for us to hold boundaries with those who have mental illness.

Chapter 5: How to Say No and Mean It

No is such a negative word. Most of the time people don't want to hear no. They want to hear only what they want to hear. When you're a people pleaser and you're saying no, many people who know you can't believe it (maybe even yourself).

Helping others is not a bad thing; it's helping others more than you can help yourself that it becomes a problem. It means neglecting yourself so that you can help others. When you neglect yourself then you aren't able to better care for others because you're not performing at 100%. When you say no, you are allowing yourself to conserve energy for a favor or task you need to do.

So, now you know how important it is to keep your boundaries and make it a point to stop always saying yes. Let's move on to actually telling people no. Up until this point we have been doing some internal reflection. Now is when we start preparing to make the changes.

When you say no, you think the world is going to come crashing down. That is mainly because no one wants to hear no. Many times, though, the fallout is almost never as serious as we think it may be. So, it's worth a shot saying no, right?

Saying no is daunting at first. I'm sure you might be thinking, "Yeah that sounds nice. But I *can't* just say no." Is that true, or do you just *think* you can't say no? Take an inventory of the times you've said yes to something, maybe to something, and no to something. Naturally you will probably have high yeses and low nos, if any, per week.

If you write down whether it was a yes or no, write what your feelings were associated with that event. Were you nervous? Was there an argument? Did it work out well? When you make the list and categorize your events in a week, you'll be able to see a pattern.

The pattern will show which questions made you automatically say yes. It'll show what you said no to and how it made you feel. More importantly, it'll tell you the types of interactions that made you stressed out. Did saying yes to your neighbor to help mow his lawn make you stressed? Was it your neighbor or mowing? Or were you too busy?

This reflection will show you the situations that you said no to and everything turned out okay. It shows you what, and whom, you can say no to in the future. It also shows you how many times you've told someone no, so you know who asks the most.

Your notes will also show you the situations where you were most pressured to say yes. It will keep you from making the same mistake in the future. When you know you're going to be in that situation then you can better prepare to say no.

Tips for Saying No

When you need to say no, there are ways you can prepare to let others down gently. The following tips can help you the next time you're in a tricky situation.

- *Stay calm. Studies show that when we are in an elevated emotional state, we are more likely to make rash, illogical decisions. When we feel pressured and panicked, we will say whatever it takes to get us out of a situation. It's human nature for our survival instinct to kick in and save us. These are the times where we reply with an automatic "yes" but come to regret it later.*

- *Don't pause too long. When you are asked something and you pause to think of an excuse, others may see this as an invitation to change your mind, because you took a second to think about it.*
- *Don't overexplain. If they are pestering you and asking why, then give them a small bit of information. You don't owe them a full-life explanation. Plus, if you start to rattle off lots of information, they may think you're lying.*
- *Come prepared with a realistic excuse. If you know someone is going to ask you to do something, think of an excuse beforehand. This keeps you from panicking when they ask.*
- *Change the subject. When someone is about to ask you something, or if they're hinting that they might need something from you, change the subject. Pick something that isn't related to what you're talking about. They can take that as a hint not to ask.*
- *Stay confident. When you say no, you need to be confident in yourself. You are choosing yourself for once and it is critical that you take time for yourself. You deserve it. If you look like you're unsure of yourself, they will continue asking and overreaching.*
- *Be honest. Being honest is always an option. It's not the end of the world to say, "I can't. I'm just too tired." If you truly have other plans, let them know that.*

- *Remember your reason for saying no. If you're too tired, remember that. If you have a lot to do the next day for a friend's birthday, say no. If you know you're going to have to back out later, say no. Remember your motivation for making yourself a priority.*

You can also use a "hard no." A hard no is a firm, "No thank you." It's short, sweet, simple, concise and clear. It doesn't leave room for the other to try and convince you to say yes. This is a big step, though, so don't be worried if you can't start here. You can use a "soft no."

A soft no is still saying no but offering a bit of explanation. Such as, "Thanks for asking, but I am just too busy this week." This is more of a transition from being a hardcore people pleaser to a more balanced giver.

Saying no can be intimidating, but it's not as bad as we think it is. Just like with anything, practice makes perfect. You can practice by understanding the difference between obligation and desire.

Difference Between Obligation and Desire

Some people say yes because they feel obligated to. Some say yes because they want to. It's important to understand the difference between wanting to and feeling like you have to. Saying yes when you *want* to means it'll be an excited "yes." Saying yes because you feel like you *must* means it'll be a reluctant "yes."

Obligation to perform a task for others feels like guilt when we say no. We feel as though it's our "job" to accept all tasks. We say yes until our plate is completely full. Then we keep saying yes.

When we continue saying yes from obligation or guilt, it can almost always lead to resentment. When you don't get as much energy in return, you feel like you've been robbed. You start to resent them for taking advantage of you and your kindness.

This is where relationships can end. Without communication among all parties, resentment leads to anger, anger leads to a breaking point, and damage is done that can't be fixed. We go from completely spending all of our time and energy on someone to never speaking to them. That's why it's so important to say yes from the heart, not the head.

If you say yes out of obligation you are going to try to find shortcuts throughout the task. You're going to want to cut corners and finish the task as quickly as possible. It doesn't matter the outcome; only how quickly you can get it done or how you can avoid it. Not only does that cheat you out of good productivity, but it cheats the person you're helping, as well.

When you start saying yes because you want to, you'll be able to see a positive shift in your life. You'll be spending time doing things you don't mind doing. You'll be helping people and you'll be happy while doing it.

Agree to requests that are similar to your likes, values, and feelings. You're going to create a stronger bond between you and the request, so you're going to do a better job. Plus, you won't use as much emotional energy. So, you can have more energy for others. It can even be energizing for some, doing tasks that they enjoy.

Even when saying yes constantly, it's important to take note of your health. You may be enjoying yourself so much that you're ignoring some important signs that you're overworked or burnt out.

Saying no may put a damper on the situation. However, you can answer in a way that keeps the conversation clear and upbeat by using positive language.

Positive Language

Positive language is a great way to improve the interactions with those around you. In everyday life we come into circumstances that can make us angry or upset. One of the first urges people pleasers get when entering this circumstance is to apologize.

When you say the words, "I'm sorry," you are admitting fault. You are agreeing that there is something wrong in the situation and you are apologizing for the outcome. That's why when some people say, "I'm sorry," others say, "It's not your fault." Those words indicate that someone is hurt or upset.

Using positive language instead allows you to open up the conversation to a better tone. For example, instead of saying, "I'm sorry I'm late," you can say, "Thank you for waiting for me." Saying thank you is a great way to show praise to the other person. Instead of downing yourself by saying I'm sorry, elevate them by using positive language when you've done wrong or failed. Instead of saying, "I'm sorry, I can't," say, "I wish I could, but I have other obligations."

Strong relationships can be built on positive language. When you're constantly using positive affirmations for others, you are keeping the energy between you balanced. When you constantly say sorry, you are giving your power to the other person.

Positive language can have a huge impact on how people perceive you. They may view you as happier, more attractive, nicer, and welcoming. People can gravitate to you because you always have positive, kind words to say. You can create a large, loyal following because you make people feel better.

Willingness to communicate and interact are shown by using positive language. People are more likely to talk to you and feel more comfortable with you when you speak this way. It also increases the chances of you being put in a cohesive and hard-working group. More people will want to work with you to get things done because of your positive outlook.

Having positive language can create an area of positivity around you. Imagine you're in a checkout line and the cash register is malfunctioning so you have to wait for a while. When you finally get to the counter, the cashier says, "Thank you for waiting, it's fixed now." Doesn't that sound better than, "Sorry it wasn't working; it wasn't my fault."

People who interact with you can leave in a better mood than before because you said thank you instead of I'm sorry. Others around you, such as coworkers, can take your idea for positive language and use it in their lives. You are indirectly affecting many people positively, just by using positive language.

Many negative phrases can be replaced with positive ones. After you practice, you'll make it a habit to use this language.

- *Instead of, "I can't help you with your request; you didn't tell me everything I needed to know"*
  - *Try, "I'd be happy to help if I could get a little more information from you."*
  - *Instead of telling someone what they didn't do, ask for what you need. You don't have to tell others that they didn't do something for*

*you when you can just ask for what you
need.*

- *Rather than "I don't know"*
  - *Try, "I can find someone who knows more
    about that."*
  - *When you want to help others, "I don't
    know" is one of the most dead-end phrases.
    If you truly want to help them, you can direct
    them to a place that they might be able to
    get the information they need.*

- *Avoid "Why does that matter?"*
  - *Practice, "What's the importance of this?" or
    "How is this related to what we are doing?"*

You can see the pattern between replacing negative language with positive. Think of phrases that may be inherently rude or negative. Think of a way to rearrange what you're saying or asking so that it sounds more positive.

Positive language allows you to say what you can do, instead of what you can't do. It shows that you care about the conversation and you are putting in effort to ensure the interaction goes well.

Bad news can be positively spun so it's easier for others to handle. Bad news can also be easier to give when using positive language. When you're not sure what to say, especially during a time of bad news, think of a few things to help you create a powerful positive phrase.

- *Bring attention to the positives in the situation.*
- *Show effort to help.*
- *Emphasize what can be done.*

- *Avoid statements that send people into a defensive mode.*
- *Show empathy, when appropriate.*

Showing empathy after all interactions involving saying no would suggest you aren't sure about your answer. When delivering bad news, however, it is better to show empathy so the receiver of the news doesn't feel attacked or alone.

You can practice using positive language every day in your life. Whether it be at work, with your family, or in public, you can use positive language.

Opportunities of Conflict

Conflict, as funny as it sounds, can open a world of opportunities. You can gain just as much as you can lose in difficult situations. You can prepare for conflict and control your actions to create positive outcomes.

When you and another person are in a conflict, you get a chance to learn more about each other. You learn how the other reacts in situations. You check out their feelings and emotions. When in conflict, if someone raises their voice, you will learn more about them by how they are reacting to this situation.

During conflict you can learn more about your conflict resolution skills. These skills govern the decisions you make and the paths you take while trying to resolve the conflict.

When you are better able to resolve conflicts with others, you are going to have a better relationship. When you know you can discuss a conflict with someone else without fighting, you are going to be more comfortable bringing up a problem with them. Communication like this leads to strong, productive, and healthy relationships.

You must use critical thinking when you are in a conflicting situation. You need to find ways out of the conflict and determine what happened to create the conflict. Thinking about how to solve the problem can be a mental exercise.

You can learn while in conflict. Have you been in problems before that you learned something you didn't know? Or you realized you were wrong? These are the times where you learn new information that you can use for similar problems in the future.

You can practice your decision-making skills while in a conflict. You have to help others decide how the conflict will turn out. You can make decisions that lead to the resolution of the problem. This gives you a sense of relief and power when the conflict ends.

Sometimes conflict leads to poor outcomes. You may decide to let go of certain people or stop certain situations that are causing you pain, discomfort, and stress. This can be a good thing. Certain relationships can be toxic over time; it doesn't matter how great it once was or how much history was shared. Conflict can give you an opportunity to get rid of the bad people and toxic energy in your life.

When you're in a conflict you have a chance to use your emotional intelligence. You may be able to notice that the other person is getting too upset so it may be time to stop talking about it for now.

You also get the opportunity to see a situation from a different viewpoint. You may both agree on a subject but not be able to tell because of different perspectives. It keeps you humble when you think you know all parts of a problem.

Standing Out

People pleasers aim to fit in. They want to make the people around them comfortable. They will say and do things to ensure they are liked by those around them and that they are leaving a good impression on others.

To start truly being yourself, you must stand out. You must stop making decisions based on the thoughts of others. You aren't helping anyone when you are holding your idea a secret, just because it's different than all of your coworkers' ideas. It's not helpful when you're not bringing up an issue with a sale because the customer would be upset.

You may aim to fit in by working late on weekdays and weekends to get others' work done. You want them to like you, so if you just finish up that project for them then you will all be friends. You overwork yourself for the thought of a benefit at the end. When in turn, the coworkers were just using you.

When you stand up for yourself, you are telling everyone what your boundaries are and what you won't allow. You are refusing to let people disrespect you and walk over you. In order to stand out, you have to be brave enough to stand up for yourself.

One fun trick to reducing anxiety and improving bravery is the Superman stance. Stand tall and puff out your chest. Put your fists on your hips and stand tall and proud like Superman. Hold this pose for about a minute or two and your body will physically start to believe you are a superhuman.

Studies show that this Superman pose can decrease anxiety because you are standing up straight and exposing your chest out to the world. This type of physical vulnerability makes you more confident in your abilities and your surroundings.

One way you can stand out is by mentioning your idea when working in a group at work or school, even if it contradicts those around you. It can be intimidating to speak up, but the group may agree with your ideas and you could contribute to a more successful group.

You can also just smile. When you smile, even if you're just smiling at yourself, your brain releases those chemicals (think back to chapter three) that make us happy. This can cause us to be actually happy, even if we were in a poor mood before.

It's important not to be egotistical when being confident. Nobody likes an egomaniac. You can be confident in your abilities and yourself without being rude or constantly announcing your confidence to others.

Chapter 6: Staying Strong

Telling people "no" can be difficult. Saying no to anyone can be difficult, but when you feel unusually pressured to say yes to people, then you might be a people pleaser.

All people pleasers have been in that situation where you weren't allowed to say no. It's the coworker that won't stop pestering you until you say yes. Or the boss that won't stop emailing you on vacation. Or the friend who begs you to do something for them, even after you've already said no.

They will make excuses for you like, "Oh, you can do that later" or "They won't mind" or "You can sleep tomorrow night." Others will go out of their way to convince you that you can do something, even when you are telling them no.

When we are fixing to tell someone no, we may feel our heart rate pick up. Our face may flush red, and we can start to sweat. We can get anxious from the possibility of upsetting others. We can be so worried about the outcomes without putting real thought into ourselves and our abilities.

Just saying no can empower us to live our own lives and control what we want to do. We don't let others, or their perceptions of us, hold us back from taking a stand in our lives. Not everyone is brave enough to do it, but you're here—so you definitely are.

Saying no holds others accountable for their actions. It is now their responsibility to find someone else who can help them or re-prioritize their agenda to be able to do the task without help.

During conversations of saying no, you can start to panic and say yes. Try to stay calm and follow some of these tips to keep you on the track to saying no and sticking with it.

1. *Remember your reason. You have a reason why you're saying no. Whether it's because you want time for yourself, energy for others, or have other plans, make sure to remind yourself the reason why you're saying no.*
2. *Focus on the positive. You may be saying no to this person, but think of what you will get from saying no. More time with your family, the opportunity to hang out with friends, do a hobby of yours, etc.*
3. *Think of your priorities. The values we discovered in chapter two have a big influence on our decisions. If the task is interfering with our values, we need to remember that when saying no.*
4. *Be polite. When you're saying no, start with gratitude for being asked. Tell them thank you for asking or you appreciate the offer but you're not able to help. Using this positive language will improve the overall interaction.*
5. *Leave. Once you've made your point, if they don't stop pressuring you, then simply leave. You can excuse yourself or tell them you have to be somewhere else. Stopping the conversation can send a stronger signal that you're not interested in their request.*

During times of trouble, there are coping mechanisms you can use to get yourself through the situation.

Coping Mechanisms

Strategies that people use when in tough situations are called coping mechanisms. Everyone has different coping mechanisms, and some may have them without knowing what they are. You can create your own coping mechanisms or practice those from others. Coping mechanisms are really great for keeping you calm in the moment.

Having a coping mechanism doesn't mean you're weak. It means you can carry yourself through a tough situation. It means you can encourage yourself without always needing others to help you. So, as you can see, coping mechanisms are helpful for emotional well-being.

There are two types of coping mechanisms. First, there are active coping methods. An active coping method means you realize the stimuli that is causing your distress and you consciously use your mechanism to relax. Second, there are the avoidant coping methods. This is when you completely avoid something that makes you uncomfortable. Some coping mechanisms are great for a short time but can be detrimental in the long run.

When a coping mechanism causes more harm than good, it's called maladaptive coping. For example, if you constantly use your avoidant mechanism for social interactions, you'll never partake in social activities. This can be detrimental to your health, work, and life.

When you have a helpful, healthy coping mechanism, then it's called an adaptive coping mechanism.

Adaptive coping methods are beneficial for appropriately handling stressful situations.

Some adaptive coping methods are:

- *Relaxation. Many relaxing activities can make it easier for people to deal with stress. Some ways you can relax include sitting in nature, meditation, listening to music, and focusing on muscle relaxation.*
- *Support. Having a support group can be critical for managing traumatic events and stress. Talking with another person or a group can help you manage stress from various situations. Having external support can prevent internalizing stress and self-isolating.*
- *Humor. Approaching and dealing with a situation through a positive light and humor can create better outcomes. Using humor can keep the situation from becoming overwhelming.*
- *Physical activity. Exercise can be one of the best ways to cope with stress. It can be a great coping mechanism for expending nervous energy and muscle tightness that comes with stress. We hold a lot of our stress in our upper body, so physical activity can allow the blood flow to improve in our tight muscles.*
- *Problem-solving. This coping mechanism is important for finding a problem that's causing you stress and trying to find a way to make it better. A problem-solving coping mechanism is beneficial for decreasing your stress and preparing for what may come.*

Some maladaptive coping mechanisms include:

- *Unhealthy self-soothing. Some self-soothing can be beneficial, but too much of any one self-soothing technique could end badly. For example, drinking alcohol, doing drugs, overeating, and excessive use of the internet or games.*
- *Risk-taking and compulsions. Stress can lead to pent-up energy. Your nervous system enacts a "fight or flight" mode that energizes your system for times of distress. Your body wants to find ways to decompress with adrenaline. You can gamble, do drugs, have unsafe sex, and more.*
- *Self-harm. Self-harming behaviors are used by people with trauma or extreme stress. Self-harm can be dangerous. If you self-harm as a coping mechanism, you should reach out to a friend, family member, or trusted medical provider as soon as you can and discuss it with them.*

People who can successfully adapt and persevere through mentally tough situations have an overall better well-being. They also have better physical, mental, and emotional health. This means that partaking in maladaptive coping mechanisms can affect the health of the entire body.

When partaking in maladaptive coping mechanisms, you are increasing the chances of anxiety, depression, and other mental health issues. Addiction is also a consequence of maladaptive coping mechanisms.

When using a substance to self-soothe, it can be beneficial in the short term. It may let you forget about your worries and focus on the fun you're having now.

However, when consistently used long-term, an addiction can form.

Make a Plan

We feel better when we go into unknown situations prepared. It can make you uneasy to not know what is going on, nor what is happening. When humans are caught off-guard it can be detrimental to our daily lives.

You can make a pre-situation plan to get prepared for saying no. When you know you're going to be asked something, try to create a plan to prepare yourself. You can relax knowing that you're prepared when someone with a request starts walking toward you.

Some of the ways you can prepare for saying no are:

- *Practice in the mirror – It may sound silly, but you can practice with yourself in a mirror. Think of how the discussion might go and practice saying no to yourself.*
- *Think of other topics to discuss beforehand – This is so that you can easily change the subject if you need to, and you could avoid topics where you might be asked for a request.*
- *Determine your coping mechanisms – Think about the environment you will be in. What are some appropriate things you can do to calm yourself?*
- *Do the Superman pose – Standing up tall with your chest pressed out can skyrocket your self-confidence. The more self-confident you are, the more likely you are to say no and stick with it.*

If you're in a situation where you feel pressured to say no, buy yourself some time. You can say things like, "Let me think about it" or "Let me get back to you." This gives you the time to relax and come back to the situation so you can say no.

You take time to thoroughly think about the request, so when you say no you are more confident in your answer. You are interrupting the "yes" cycle and allowing yourself the liberty of thinking before you answer. Giving yourself more time before answering gets you the confidence to say no every time.

In many situations, you and the other person can come to a compromise. The only time where you will want to make a compromise is if you want to do the request, but you only have so much time and ability to finish the task. You can both come to an agreement on how the task will be done that makes you both happy. Don't compromise if you really want, or need, to say no.

In other situations, you must wing it. You have to listen to their response and reply appropriately. You don't have to completely shut them out after saying no. They may have additions to the request that you would be interested in.

Your coworkers may understand when you say no and explain why they asked. This can benefit you because you can see why people feel comfortable asking you for things. You can see if there is a pattern between the person who is asking and what they are asking for.

People associate the word "no" with rejection. Some cannot understand the difference between refusal and rejection. Understanding the difference between these two can prevent problems. Refusal is simply stating no—that you cannot help at this time. Rejection means a strong no and an insinuation not to ask again.

When you refuse a request, you are simply saying no to what they need done. You may think you're rejecting them, but you're not. You're simply refusing to help them with what they need.

Many times, people will understand that your refusal is not personal and simply what needs to be done. Others may think that you're being rude. Remember, it's ultimately their problem—not yours.

Don't give in to bullying, bribery, flirtation, or flattery. People will say and do anything they need to in order to get your help. Don't believe everything you hear from some who is asking you for something.

Sometimes people need to be told no. Constantly being told yes doesn't allow for anyone to develop self-control. They won't take responsibility for their actions because they think it's someone else's fault.

Because they've asked someone else to do something for them, they are placing the responsibility on someone else. That way if they fail, it won't be their fault, in their minds. In this sense, telling them no reminds them that there are some things that just have to be done themselves.

Support

People pleasers can have low self-esteem. Our self-esteem is the opinion we have of ourselves. When we have a positive opinion of ourselves, we have a positive outlook on life. Having a positive outlook lets us deal with the struggles that we face every day.

When we have low self-esteem, we have a more negative outlook on life. We tend to view things and situations as acts against us, rather than completely separate events. When we dwell on ourselves with low self-esteem, we see things negatively. This makes us even weaker when trying to fight off stress and issues.

Support is a critical way of staying strong while saying no. It can keep you grounded and conscious when in times of distress. Support can come in many forms, such as:

- *Physical support*
- *Emotional support*
- *Mental support*
- *Financial support*
- *Self-support*
- *Support from friends and family*
- *Support from a therapist/counseling*

When we ask others for help, we are making ourselves a priority. We have to take care of ourselves. If we aim to help others as much as we want, we have to take care of ourselves or we won't have any help to give. At that point, our exhaustion will take over our wants and needs.

You can create a support journal to keep yourself focused when you need it. In this journal you can write times when you're inspired, times when you feel like you've succeeded, nice things about yourself, nice things others have said about you, and more.

Take this journal and place it in a spot that you'll see it every day or have easy access to it. When you're feeling discouraged, you can look at this journal and read all of the nice things about yourself. This is an immediate boost of support.

Handling Reactions

Obviously, we always assume the worst in a situation (shout-out to anxiety). We are sure that our entire lives are going to crumble if we say no. Or if we act a certain way. Or do a certain thing. Ninety percent of the time that's not the case. It's just our imagination.

However, there is that ten percent where you will receive a rough reaction when you do something that isn't a big people-pleaser. If you are surrounded with people who love and understand you, you are less likely to get a negative reaction. If you do get a negative reaction, it isn't the end of the world. Especially when you know how to react appropriately.

Being emotionally intelligent will help you when you're in these situations where things can get heated quickly.

<u>Emotional Intelligence</u>

Emotional intelligence is the ability to understand, manage, and use our own emotions to relieve stress in positive ways, empathize with others, communicate effectively, defuse conflict, and overcome challenges.

Emotional intelligence helps us create strong relationships, achieve personal and career goals, and succeed at work and school. This intelligence allows you to better connect with your feelings, make informed decisions, and turn intentions to actions.

There are four parts that make up emotional intelligence:

1. *Self-awareness: This means you can recognize your emotions and the effects they are having on your behavior, words, actions, and thoughts. You understand your weaknesses and strengths.*
2. *Self-management: Self-management means you're able to recognize and control your behaviors and*

feelings. You can take initiative, adapt to circumstances that are changing, follow through on commitments, and manage emotions healthier.
3. *Social awareness: Social awareness means having empathy. You can understand the needs, concerns, and emotions of other people. You can pick up on emotional cues, recognize the dynamics of power in an organization, and feel comfortable socially.*
4. *Relationship management: You can maintain good relationships after developing them. You can inspire and influence others, manage conflict, work well in a team, and communicate clearly.*

Emotional intelligence is so important because it affects many parts of our health and daily lives. Emotional intelligence can affect:

- *Your quality of work at your job or school. Having high emotional intelligence is beneficial for understanding the changing environment of your workplace. You can use your emotional intelligence to motivate and lead others and earn that big promotion.*
- *Your mental health. When you cannot control your emotions, it can lead to feelings (and even diagnosis) of anxiety and depression. It'll be hard to establish strong relationships if you're not familiar or comfortable with your expressions and emotions.*
- *Your physical health. If you are having trouble controlling your emotions, you probably have trouble controlling your stress. Uncontrolled stress can have so many problems on the body, including digestive issues, early death, stroke,*

high blood pressure, fluctuations in blood sugar, pain, insomnia, exhaustion, inability to fight colds and infections, acne, weight gain, low sex drive, headaches, muscle tension, and much more.

- ○ *One of the first steps of improving emotional intelligence is learning to manage stress effectively.*

- *Your social intelligence. Being one with your emotions allows you to connect with those, and the environments, surrounding you. Social intelligence gives you the ability to understand the difference between those who are trying to help you and those who are trying to hurt you. You can feel happier and more loved, understand another person's feelings for you, and balance the nervous system during social interactions when you have high social intelligence.*

- *Your relationships. Your relationships can be affected by emotional intelligence by helping you understand how to better express your emotions to loved ones. You can also better understand the feelings of others. That way you can create stronger relationships everywhere you go.*

As you can see, emotional intelligence is just about vital for everyday functions. Those who refuse to listen, blame others, and constantly argue may have low emotional intelligence. If you're afraid you have low emotional intelligence, don't worry. There are many ways you can improve your emotional intelligence.

<u>First, work on your self-management</u>. Think of a time where you were very overwhelmed by a situation or a decision. Did you make the right call? Do you agree that it was hard to come to a clear decision during that time

because of so much stress? It's easier to make decisions when we aren't overwhelmed by our emotions.

Working on your self-management improves emotional intelligence because you're able to understand your emotions. You can recognize your emotions as you transition through them. This allows you to control the emotion, rather than letting the emotion control you.

When emotions control us, we can make illogical decisions. We are thinking in a fight-or-flight mode and doing and saying anything we can to survive the situation (if we are scared). If we're happy we may make manic decisions, such as shopping or binge eating. If we're angry we can punch walls and break things if our emotion controls us.

When you can learn to stay present in a situation, you can better understand unpopular information. This way, you can cap your emotions before they bubble over and start affecting your thoughts and actions.

Having a handle on our emotions allows us to adapt to changing environments. If you are getting criticism at work, you can accept the information with an open mind, rather than forming a defense mechanism.

<u>Second, focus on your self-awareness</u>. Now, this sounds similar to self-management, but it means being able to understand *why* we are having these emotions. Our self-awareness means we understand our own character, feelings, desires, and motives.

Your management of core feelings, like sadness, joy, fear, and anger, can be based on some of your first life experiences. If, as a baby, your primary parent valued and understood your emotions, it's more likely now that your emotions are valuable in your adult life.

However, if your emotional experiences came from a threatening, painful, or confusing time as a child, then there's a bigger chance you aim to keep distance between you and your emotions.

It's important to connect to emotions so you can understand how your emotions are influencing your brain. You may think of something awful to say if you're angry. You may think of doing something scary when you're sad.

Self-awareness allows us to understand that we are having these thoughts because we are angry, or because we are sad. The decisions we make under these emotions have an effect on the outcome.

Third, build your social awareness. Social awareness gives you the opportunity to interpret and recognize the (mostly) nonverbal cues that other people are constantly doing. You can "read the room." This means you understand the overall emotion of the room and you don't say or do something that would be emotionally inappropriate.

You can read these nonverbal cues from different people. Some give off more than others. Some don't even know they're using them. They are simply acting as they do normally. Focusing on nonverbal cues can teach you a lot about a person, and the room around you.

Nonverbal cues are important for determining a person's true feelings. If they say they're not anxious, but they're picking at their nails and biting their lip, they are more than likely nervous. If someone says they're not angry, but their tone is off and their face is red, they might be angry.

There are many types of nonverbal cues, such as:

- *Body language*
- *Eye contact*
- *Posture*
- *Facial expressions*
- *Tone of voice*
- *Appearance*
- *Nodding or shaking the head*
- *Movement and gestures*

These nonverbal cues can be read to determine someone's mood as it changes. If a man is making a woman laugh, she may have her arms open or be standing near him. Suddenly, if he makes her uncomfortable, you would be able to see her cross her arms in front of her chest and step away from him.

You can learn a lot about groups of people. When you see the way that others act, you understand the power dynamics of the group. You can read the social environment to learn more about the group than what they can tell you. You can share emotional experiences with the group, showing you're socially comfortable and empathetic.

Nonverbal cues are very important for a thorough connection and relationship. You can connect with people on a deeper level when you can uncover things about them that they may not tell you. You may even be able to pick up on emotions that they may not be conscious of.

Mindfulness is beneficial for social and emotional awareness. Being mindful means being in the present. You're not zoning off on your phone, you're not stuck in your head, nor are you thinking about other things. Your thoughts and senses are absorbed with what is happening right now. When you're tuned in to other things, you're unable to pick up on the nonverbal cues that are going on in the room and interactions around you.

While multitasking is very beneficial, it can take away from your ability to pick up on the nonverbal cues that are showing changes in emotion in those around you. If you're not keeping up with the emotions in the room, you could say or do something inappropriate.

When you focus on your interaction and set all other thoughts aside, you can reach your social goals. If you want to make a friend out of someone, you need to talk to them without being occupied by other thoughts. Or else the relationship may not be as strong.

<u>Lastly, to improve emotional intelligence, you want to improve your relationship management.</u> Relationship management starts with learning to understand what others are experiencing.

Not only is watching for nonverbal cues important, watching for your own nonverbal cues is important for relationship management. The muscles in our face respond to our emotions, even if we don't. Our facial expressions will mimic our emotions and thoughts, even if we aren't conscious of it.

It's impossible to stop these abrupt reactions from our emotions. Sometimes you can catch yourself when you are making a face, or when you know you're about to make one, you can look away. Think of crying. This is an automatic reaction that we can't stop sometimes. Recognizing and improving our nonverbal cues can help us manage our facial expressions and make better friends.

Relationship management includes understanding what others are feeling and how they are experiencing their surroundings. This improves your ability to "read the room." Reading the room means understanding the overall tone of the room and not doing anything that would be considered inappropriate at the time.

You can improve your relationships with humor. Humor allows the body to laugh, reduce stress, return the nervous system back to normal, and improves your empathy for others.

Every human relationship will encounter conflict. Whether it's big or small, conflicts are a normal, common part of life. Conflict can be an opportunity for us to grow into something bigger and better. Conflict can elevate our mindset to a place that we didn't think of at first.

Seeing conflict as an opportunity for improvement allows us to be less aggressive and angry when we encounter conflict. If we desensitize our brains to the negative aspects of conflicts, we can better work through problems without them ruining our relationships.

Chapter 7: Expressing Yourself

Self-expression is one of the most important ways we connect and grow with each other. When we show deep down who we are, we can create stronger, more authentic relationships.

Let's talk about the values we found in chapter two. What did you discover about yourself? Were you surprised by your answers? Did you know what the top three were before you even started?

If we aren't sure of our passions, then we can get distracted from daily activities with frustrations. We can ask ourselves questions like, "Why am I doing this?" and "How is this important to me?"

Expressing yourself feels great. Think of a time where you created something, or fixed it, or completed a project that you were so proud of. Remember the inner smile you got while standing back and looking at your accomplishment.

Do you remember the energy you felt when finishing? You felt on top of the world. You told yourself you were proud, and you would keep doing those things to make you feel like that. But people-pleasing got in the way.

Suddenly that event isn't fun anymore. You don't feel like you're a part of the process and you're just going through routines. You've lost the spark you once had.

When you express yourself, you are allowing your creativeness to take control. You acknowledge the fact that being creative means you are consistently told no. When you've thought of something that others can't understand yet, it can lead to fear and confusion. Most of the time people will reject the creativeness because it can cause discomfort.

That's why people pleasers don't express themselves. They don't want the spotlight and they don't want to step on toes. People pleasers often believe that by expressing themselves they are taking room and attention away from others' expressions. They would rather others be able to voice their opinions and ideas.

If you can find creative outlets for your expression, you can improve your self-confidence. When you do things that you enjoy, you're expressing yourself. Expressing yourself is easier said than done. Some people don't know how. That's okay if you don't. We are going to cover some tips on how you can express yourself easier.

Activities

Activities can be a great way to express yourself. The great thing about doing things that stimulate your mind is that they cause you to think. You think of new ideas, and old ideas, and create something you're proud of.

Some activities that can be beneficial for expressing yourself include:

- *Painting*
- *Photography*
- *Exercise*
- *Writing*
- *Design (in fashion, architecture, interior design, etc.)*
- *Dancing*
- *Drawing*
- *Construction*
- *Baking or Cooking*

During an activity of expressing yourself, you can go into the zone. When you're in the zone, nothing else matters. You are enjoying yourself and you're able to make your dreams come to life. You're not focused on what's going on around you. Instead, you're focusing on what's right in front of you.

When you're in the zone, that's how you know you're expressing yourself. You may be moving so fluidly and getting a lot of work done. You can be so infatuated with what's going on in front of you that you don't notice your surroundings.

Social

Being social can allow you to express yourself, and vice versa. When you talk about your passion, you are expressing yourself. When talking about your passion, your eyes can widen, your tone can increase, and you tend to move around more.

In social settings, being a good conversationalist can be beneficial for making friends and having a better time. When you're shy, though, it can be harder to put yourself out there, let alone express yourself.

Many times, being a people pleaser sounds like being shy. It's like one-word answers because you're scared to answer out. Shyness is also like being a people pleaser because you say what needs to be said to avoid uncomfortable interactions.

When others around you are talking freely and expressing themselves, you can be envious of their attention or even angry with them for acting out on their desires when you can't. You may even feel inadequate, which can lead to feelings of depression, humiliation, and isolation.

When learning to express yourself in social situations, it's important to remember the list below.

- *Fake it.* You need to pretend you're the most social person you know. You talk to everyone you see. That cashier at the coffee shop? Ask them what their favorite drink is. Your coworker? Ask them if they have weekend plans.
- *Take a class.* This can be cooking, painting, sculpture, etc. This way, you don't have to stress yourself out trying to find something to talk about. You can talk about what you're doing.
- *Keep a positive attitude.* Don't wear yourself out stressing so much for the social interaction that you don't have any energy left when it comes time. Keeping a positive attitude will make a more positive outcome.
- *Don't get down on yourself.* Did you misspeak or stumble on your words? It's okay! Everyone does it. Take a deep breath and get back out there. Don't take yourself out of the game and lecture yourself. Finish the quarter with a slam dunk.
- *Smile.* When you smile, not only do you look happier, but you'll actually feel happier! You also look more approachable to others.
- *Practice.* You can find a neutral topic that you like to discuss and make mental notes of what you can talk about. You can run the conversation over with a friend before trying it out on others.
- *Repeat.* Once you have had a positive social interaction, go for another one. After you have left a positive social experience then you feel energized.

- _Use a story._ *Do you have a funny situation that has happened to you once? You can use this story as an icebreaker. You listen for a relevant part in the conversation that would fit in with your story, pause for an opportunity to speak, then tell it.*

Self-expression can be extremely beneficial for our health. Our brain reacts in certain ways to process self-expression. The healthy brain reactions and constant creativeness from self-expression can prevent depression, dementia, and many more illnesses.

One of the best ways to express ourselves is through conversation. Conversation can be life changing. Whether it's a self-help seminar that's two hours long, or a brief conversation while waiting on the bathroom, we can be touched by conversation with others.

Receptors of conversation are usually more affected by conversation than those who are talking. That doesn't mean the one speaking won't be affected by the conversation, simply that they are not as often affected as those being talked to.

Brain Changes During Self-Expression

When you're able to listen to someone else without judgement, you can trigger your prefrontal cortex. The prefrontal brain is called the executive brain. The prefrontal cortex is located on the front of the brain, behind the forehead and eyes.

The prefrontal cortex is responsible for personality expression, decision-making, planning cognitive behaviors that are complex, and much more. The prefrontal cortex is associated with actions and thoughts regarding our inner goals. These are basically our executive functions (hence calling it the executive brain).

Executive function includes:

- *Ability to understand differences in conflicting thoughts*
- *Understand the differences between better and best*
- *Differences between same and different*
- *Differences between good and bad*
- *Understanding consequences of our actions*
- *Goal orientation*
- *Concentration*
- *Reasoning*
- *Judgement*
- *Creativity*
- *Abstract thinking*
- *Organization*
- *Emotional regulation*
- *Interpretation of reality*
- *Predicting outcomes*
- *Social control*
- *Ability to suppress actions that could lead to socially unacceptable behavior*

As you can see, the prefrontal cortex includes just about every thought and behavior we need to create and maintain healthy relationships. It's because the prefrontal cortex is critical for our sense of self. When we know who we are, we can create more authentic relationships.

The prefrontal cortex is divided into two parts: the left and the right. The left is associated with positive goals, emotions, and approach. The right side focuses on negative emotions and avoidance. The left side also has more dopamine activity and receptors like we get from rewards and motivation. The right side is more associated with anxiety and has higher norepinephrine activity.

People who have a prejudice toward positive emotions may have more activation in their left prefrontal cortex. More activation in the right prefrontal cortex shows more experience with negative emotions.

In people who have depression, their right prefrontal cortex may be overactive when compared to the left side. Less access to the left (positive) side can mean that people with depression have a harder time connecting with positive goal-oriented behavior and thought. Not to mention, more activity in the positive side includes more activity for punishment, since the left side is associated with rewards and motivation.

When we express ourselves, we are triggering a response in our prefrontal cortex that shows we are creative and goal oriented. Activity in the prefrontal cortex increases, which means you've got more creativity and abstract thoughts.

Serotonin, dopamine, and oxytocin are hormones that are released when we are doing something we enjoy, especially with others. When we say no, we can take the time for ourselves and what we want to do. This makes us happier. So, our brains give out these chemicals.

When we don't let others dictate our words and actions, we are making a decision to express ourselves. This can give us an adrenaline rush of positive energy. We can feel free, like we've finally taken off a mask to take a deep breath of fresh air.

Not only do these chemicals make us happy, but they also have many beneficial effects on the body.

Serotonin:

1. *Helps regulate and reduce moods, anxiety, and depression*
2. *Can help heal wounds*
3. *Maintains bone health*
4. *Helps control bowel movements*
5. *Can control and affect sleep*

Dopamine:

1. *Helps regulate mood*
2. *Improves memory and focus*
3. *Affects movement*
4. *Plays a role in depression and anxiety*
5. *Plays a role in psychosis*

Oxytocin:

1. *Improves recognition*
2. *Promotes trust*
3. *Plays a role in sexual and reproductive health*
4. *Improves attachments with each other*
5. *Increases bonding*

When we choose to express ourselves, we are choosing happiness. We are choosing what we want and when we want it. Expressing yourself is one way you can benefit from these chemicals.

Can't you agree that after a positive social engagement or interaction we feel energized? It's like we've had a reset and had a whole change of mind. You feel happier. These chemicals are responsible for the energy we feel.

Ways to Express Yourself

Being able to express yourself in healthy ways allows you to live a more fulfilling and authentic life. You're able to be your true self, making you more confident. It's easier to release emotions, believe in yourself, and create a life you want when expressing yourself.

There are many ways you can express yourself.

1. *Self-expression is when you can demonstrate and clearly communicate your honest feelings. This is important for helping you find out who you are, what you like, and what you don't like. This gives you more experience dealing with various emotions.*
2. *Acknowledge your emotions. Be aware of how they are affecting you. It can be hard to honor and listen to our emotions. Some people may not know how to appropriately express their emotions. It's easy for us to hide our emotions or stuff them away.*
   - *It's common to be ashamed or embarrassed by emotions. But acknowledging your emotions can allow you to channel the energy into something great, rather than nervous or confused energy.*
3. *Decorate for an event. Decorating can be a great way to show your creative side. It allows you to design areas, colors, patterns, shapes, sizes, and much more. Dealing with all of these aspects allows you to think with many parts of the brain. This allows you to use more energy in expressing yourself through decoration.*
4. *Paint. Painting is a great way to understand your emotions in real time. Think of what you want to paint. Think of the color scheme you want to use. Is*

it a bright color group? You might be feeling happy or excited. Is it more blues and purples? You could be relaxed or even sad.

5. <u>*Try something new.*</u> *When you're learning something new, you're able to try something you haven't before. This introduces your mind, body, and thoughts to unfamiliar territory. This gives you an opportunity to take advantage of the unfamiliarity and express yourself through the new activity.*

6. <u>*Dance.*</u> *Your emotions can create nervous energy. Your emotions not only affect your thinking, but also your body. Your muscles will be affected by your emotions as well. When you're happy, your muscles are comfortable and ready to move! When you're stressed, they may be tense or tremble.*

   - *When you dance, you let your body move however it wants. You let it flow with the music and move as fast or slow as you want. You can express yourself and your emotions through your movements.*

7. <u>*Go on a vacation.*</u> *You can find somewhere new across the world and go there. You will be submerged into a new experience and you can try new things. That way you are more cultured and well-rounded.*

8. <u>*Make a friend.*</u> *When you meet a new friend, you're able to connect with them on a personal level. You can express yourself to them to make a stronger friendship.*

9. <u>*Change your wardrobe.*</u> *One of the best ways you can express yourself is through your clothing. You can mix colors, textiles, patterns, and more.*

10. <u>*Get a pet.*</u> *Believe it or not, you can confide in your pets like you would someone else. It will allow you*

to talk through your thoughts, rather than obsessing over them alone in your head.

By now, I'm sure you get the picture of what you can do to express yourself. When you're more confident with expressing yourself, you're more able to say no assertively.

Chapter 8: Being Assertive

As a people pleaser, we have certainly become the victim of a "please, please, please" request. We didn't actually want to do it, but because we were begged to do it, we finally gave in and said yes. It doesn't matter how many times we say no, someone can beg until we collapse under the pressure.

When people beg, it can cause us stress and irritation. We can't think clearly because we know someone is going to keep asking us for something. It can negatively affect our performance and relationships.

When we're assertive, we're able to say no and mean it. We can get our point across without being rude about it. Being assertive allows us to say no and not have to worry about people begging us.

Being assertive means standing up for what you and others believe in through a positive and firm standpoint. Being assertive also means not just accepting what is wrong because it is the norm.

Being assertive is a very important communication skill. It can help you stand up for your point and express yourself without affecting the beliefs and rights of others. Your self-esteem will be boosted by your assertiveness, as well as respect for you from others. While some people are naturally assertive, you can also learn to be more assertive.

It's important to be assertive as a people pleaser because when you say no, you need to mean it. If you are trying to stay strong but someone just keeps hassling you about it, now is the time to plant a firm no, without causing conflict.

When you're successfully assertive, you're able to get your point across without hurting or upsetting yourself or others. Being assertive includes being emotionally intelligent enough to know when you might make others upset.

Passive, Assertive, and Aggressive

Let's talk for a second about the differences between passive, aggressive, and assertive. People pleasers tend to bend their will to the wants and needs of others. This means they verbally agree with others even when they don't actually agree with them. This also includes agreeing with something even if we know it's wrong.

People pleasers feel that if they act assertive then others will think they are being aggressive. They think that if they push against anyone or their opinions in the slightest way, then they will be disliked and shunned from the group.

When people are passive, they let others walk all over them. They don't stand up for what's right, others, or themselves. Being passive means volunteering your voice to be sacrificed for the comfort of the group.

Being too passive keeps you from getting taken seriously. Even if you do and say what needs to be done for others to like you, people can see this, and they may not trust you. They think you might tell them what they want to hear instead of the truth. Being passive can also decrease happiness, self-confidence, and self-expression.

Being assertive means getting your message across without upsetting anyone. You are clear and concise in your delivery. It's the perfect combination of polite but stern. You're not being rude or "sucking up" to someone.

Being too assertive can mean you are an obstacle for progress. When you are hell-bent on getting your idea across, you can't listen to others and what they're saying. You can't be empathetic to others because you're involved with yourself.

In this situation, it can be helpful to be passive. You can agree to disagree and work toward a solution as a team. You may not accept the resolution, but you should be able to commit to moving forward with the decision to assist your colleagues.

Aggression is when someone speaks through gritted teeth, at a piercing tone, or loudly. Being aggressive is walking toward anyone, using your arms in a wild motion, and being overall angry with your message delivery.

Being too aggressive can lead to constant conflict, enemies, isolation, anger, resentment, and much more. It can create a threatening atmosphere that no one wants to be around. There is a difference between being feared and being respected. Instilling anger and fear in others creates resentment, not loyalty.

When others are being aggressive, there are techniques you can use to get out of the situation.

1. ***Talk to a manager.*** *If you feel like someone is being aggressive toward you, speaking with a trusted advisor or Human Resources manager can help resolve the problem.*
2. ***Use your words.*** *Try to talk them out of the situation. You can change the subject or say things like, "Why don't we talk about something else?"*
3. ***Acknowledge their feelings and explain the situation.*** *You can tell them, "I see you're upset. Why don't we talk more about this when we have all calmed down?"*

4. ***Talk to them.*** *A coworker may seem aggressive because they're stressed out or concerned over other situations. Sometimes other people's attitudes have nothing to do with us and more to do with them. Talking to them can determine if there's anything that can be done to help them with their aggression.*

5. ***Learn more about them.*** *Someone may be aggressive toward you because they don't know you or they feel threatened by you. Learn more about them and you could find ways to connect with them.*

6. ***Use your emotional intelligence.*** *Try to understand why they're upset. Attempt to see the situation from their point of view so you can be empathetic. Pay attention to them so they don't get overly upset. Things can be said and done that can never be taken back.*

7. ***Leave the situation.*** *If you're feeling uncomfortable and truly threatened, end the conversation and leave immediately. You do not have to offer an explanation. Simply stand up and walk out of the room or building.*

8. ***Stay calm.*** *If you were to get aggressive to match them, it could lead to more trouble. If you're not able to have self-control, then it can cause just as much trouble for you as it can for them.*

Being assertive is designed on mutual respect. It can be considered a diplomatic and effective communication style. It's a form of self-respect. Assertiveness shows that you are aware of others' rights and feelings. It shows you're willing to work with others to find a solution to problems.

It's not only *what* you say that's important, but also *how* you say it. Assertive communication is respectful and direct. When you're too passive or too aggressive people are more focused on your delivery than what you're saying.

Confident, Clear, and Controlled

The key to being successfully assertive is being confident, clear, and controlled. Communication is key for everything we do and every decision we make. Not only does it matter *what* we are communicating, but also *how* we are communicating it.

When you're in business you are going to interact with many people. Some will be insecure and won't speak up for themselves; others are going to be egotistical and won't allow anyone else to get a word in. Some may even have short tempers.

When these people, on either side, overtake the room, then there will be no constructive conversations. One half will do all the talking while the other half sits in silence. This decreases creativity and performance.

Communication must be productive and respectful. Communication must also be equal and fair to be successful. One person cannot speak for the other. You must use charisma, insight, emotional control, and courage to speak your ideas and stand behind them.

Be prepared for what happens after you express your opinions. It won't always go your way. You have to remember to be confident in yourself to handle any situation that might come.

Being confident means standing on your own in the face of an obstacle, fear, or challenge. Confidence is key to getting a lot of things in life and improving your overall happiness.

Be prepared to deliver the entire message when you've got their attention. You are being clear about what you want, so they are ready to hear it all. When they retaliate with criticism, questions, and thoughts, you have to be prepared to follow through with that same confidence you had when you started. Being direct will help you react in these situations. Be direct and clear on your point—that way it leads them straight to it.

When others contradict you or question your ideas and opinions, they are challenging you. Don't view this as a rejection, but rather an opportunity to argue your side. This makes you strengthen your testimony. View these discussions as opportunities to talk through your ideas. This way you can prevent becoming aggressive or defensive.

Becoming aggressive or defensive may suggest that you're not confident in your thoughts and you feel the need to lash out. When someone comes to you with other information, take a look from their point of view. Then calmly try to explain how and why you see it differently.

Directness and clarity give authority and power when you're trying to converse with others. But be sure to understand the difference between bold and obnoxious. Bold can draw attention and respect; being obnoxious can cause others to be offput by you.

Being assertive includes getting your ideas across clearly. You want others to be able to see your point of view and actually take you seriously. To do that, you must communicate your ideas clearly.

Conversation and communication in the workplace are critical for business. It can be intimidating to tell others your thoughts and ideas. You may be afraid of the outcome or what they might think. However, being assertive will ensure that you are taken seriously.

When you're clear on what you want and need, people are more open to listening to you with interest. They don't spend their time trying to figure out what it is that you want. They can spend their time and mental energy focusing on what you're saying.

If you're wanting to pitch an idea to a boss or higher-up, you may only have a certain amount of time. So, you can't tell them everything you want to tell them. What you can do, though, is create and practice your information.

Determine the top three points associated with your plan or idea and how it can benefit others or the organization. You want to get them hooked with the vital information; that way they ask questions, and it gives you the opportunity to tell them all about your idea and opinion. By getting directly to the point, people aren't getting a watered-down edition of your idea.

Being assertive is more successful when you're giving your thoughts in a controlled manner. Yelling and cursing won't get the point across any faster than just having a conversation.

You can give your thoughts and opinions in a calm but strong tone. When you're open-minded and cooperative, you create conversations that lead to solutions and productivity. Being controlled by yourself in the workplace keeps you from lashing out and starting trouble, when it can be thought through. Controlling your tone and reactions improves the outcome of interactions with coworkers.

Once you give them the critical points, they will be hooked for more information. This is your chance to tell them the details that were left out during the pitch. Not only are you giving them more information, but you have piqued their interest to want to know more.

Especially with higher executives, people in business appreciate thought-provoking questions. This means challenging thoughts and being challenged. These challenges are what create the new ideas and opportunities that we have.

Passive	Assertive	Aggressive
"I don't mind what we do."	"We need to do it this way because it'll help all of us."	"We are doing it this way, no need to keep talking about it."
"I guess I can handle another project."	"I'm too busy right now, but thanks for asking."	"I said I'm not doing it, don't ask me again."
"I'm sorry for being late."	"Thank you for waiting."	"Kevin is always late, so who cares if I am?"
"I don't have an opinion."	"Here is what I think. . . "	"I don't like it, so we're not doing it."

Building a Better Mental Health

Our mental health is critical to every aspect of our lives. Our mental health can control whether or not we do something, how we do it, when, and much more. When we have solid mental health, we can be more confident and prepared to be assertive.

Mental health plays a role in being assertive because being assertive requires clear thoughts and confidence. When you're being assertive, you need to be clear about your points. You can't be clear about your points when you're not able to be clear about your thoughts.

Being confident assists in being assertive because you believe in yourself enough to stand up for what you believe in. You are confident in your abilities to handle whatever may come next. Having a healthy mental state lets you be more confident in yourself.

You can build a better mental health in many ways. You can learn how to find the things that are causing stress and remove them. This will not only take away stress, but it'll make you happier and healthier.

You can't be successfully assertive when you're stressed out. If you're stressed, your body is exhausted. You feel like you could cry at any second. You need a break if you've reached this point. But if you're too stressed to hold your own in the face of a challenge, it's time to regroup.

When you're determining things that cause you stress, there are a few lists and tricks you can make to find some of the parts of your life that stress you out the most. Now, many of you may automatically be thinking of things that stress you out. You may also have things that cause you stress that you don't know about.

Let's talk about some ways to determine what's giving you stress.

1. *What are your nightmares about? You can tell a lot about yourself through understanding your nightmares. During times of severe stress, the body can manifest the nervous thoughts and energy into nightmares. Do you have nightmares about getting fired? Or being naked during a big presentation? Maybe you're worried about how you're doing at work.*
2. *What are your feelings when you first encounter something? For example, when someone asks you about your job, do you automatically get a feeling of excitement and happiness? Or stress and exhaustion?*
     a. *What are your feelings when you first walk into a room? Do you get distracted by a pile of dirty clothes on the floor, or dishes in the sink? When you encounter discomfort when talking about something, it may be causing you some stress.*
3. *Do you realize you're having a better time with some friends than others? Why is that? Maybe one friend is causing you more stress than you realize.*
4. *Is there a thought, event, or situation that you keep pushing off? You may be telling yourself you're too busy and you can't get it done. You may even see it as procrastination. It could be avoidance. That situation can be bringing you stress so you're avoiding it.*
5. *Is there a big event or a specific date/anniversary coming up?*

The more we learn about ourselves, the more we can determine what is stressing us out. We will be able to recognize these experiences of stress and where it is coming from. We will know where our stress is coming from at that moment and work toward making it better.

Once you've found things that are stressing you out, determine if they are worth keeping in your life. Is an estranged friendship giving you anxiety? It may be time to move forward with your life. Is your job affecting your health? It might be time to start looking for something else.

Getting rid of these stresses can improve your mental health significantly. This is just one way that you can water your mental garden. Some other ways include:

- *Meditation*

  - *Meditation is a great way to ground yourself in the moment. It allows you to focus on one thing that is in the present. You don't think about the future or past, just what is right now. This is calming to the body because you are relaxed and in a calming atmosphere.*

- *Exercise*

  - *Exercise can be a great way to improve your mental health. Your brain physically benefits from exercise by excreting hormones and increasing blood flow. You also feel more confident after working out because of the hormones, so you have less chance of severe symptoms from anxiety and depression.*

- *Spa/massage days*

  - *Pamper yourself regularly. It can be a massage every month or a manicure every Thursday. Giving yourself that special time and focus each week gives you the chance to focus on yourself. This boosts your self-love and your self-confidence, both of which are a critical part of positive mental health.*

- *Journaling*

  - *Almost all stress we have is caused by ourselves and our brains. When we journal, we can get all of the information out of our heads and onto paper. Once we do that, we feel like we can relax because we let go of what we've been holding onto.*

- *Creativity*

  - *Get your brain blood flowing. While you're thinking and moving, you're distracted with what you're doing now. Focusing on something other than what is bothering you will decrease your stress.*

- *Organization*

  - *When we have clutter, it takes a lot for our brain to process everything at once. It's a lot of stimuli that can make us anxious. Our heads are consistently trying to zone in on each item and process what it is. This is exhausting and can take away from your life.*

- *Having a good diet*

  - *Having a good diet is beneficial for physical health; why wouldn't it be beneficial for mental health? Fresh fruits and vegetables improve the function of the brain in many ways. Cutting out sugar is also very beneficial for physical and mental health.*

Creating a better mental health sets you up for success in all areas of your life.

Chapter 9: What if Nothing is Working?

It can be stressful making life changes. I mean, you could've just found out that you're a people pleaser. Maybe you knew you were a people pleaser and you just now found out how hard it is on yourself.

It is common to fail when trying something new. You are doing something different than what you normally do. Not only does this mean breaking our own norms, but it also means putting ourselves in uncomfortable, vulnerable positions so we can grow and change.

Our brain makes it a habit to say yes. So we could fail right in the beginning just because that's what we're used to doing: saying yes, all the time. We have to break the routine in our minds before we can try to change it.

Once we've broken it, we have to "unlearn" our previous behavior and train to learn the new behavior. Taking knowledge and updating it allows us to change our thoughts and mindsets. It sounds easier than it is, but with patience and practice you'll get the hang of it in no time.

If you're trying to stop being a people pleaser but you keep failing, remember that it means you're trying. If you're not trying, then you're not failing. Failing just shows your dedication and determination to return and do even better.

When you're trying to stop being a people pleaser, and you're making changes to your behavior, there are some things that can go wrong.

1. *Your fake relationships can crumble. Once these people see that you're living for yourself now, they may have no interest in continuing the friendship with you.*

2. *Your boss and coworkers can get angry. They're not used to you turning down projects or extra work. They are used to you doing the work of three people. This can cause a stir in your work relationships, but only momentarily.*

3. *People in your personal life could be confused, angry, or upset with you. They're used to having you pander to them and what they want. They may have an initial knee-jerk reaction to react badly. You are making a change, so try to be patient with them (as long as they are worth it).*

4. *Guilt. In the beginning you're going to experience a lot of guilt. Guilt for changing. Guilt for saying no. You may start feeling like you're not helpful. But there's a difference between being helpful and being taken advantage of. You can be helpful without being a complete people pleaser.*

If you find yourself hitting these obstacles and you cave eventually, don't panic. We can learn some time management skills to make sure you get everything done. When you limit your time, you can spend it wisely. You'd be surprised how much time you can find throughout the day when you don't waste it.

Time Management

Let's talk about some tips and tricks for time management.

1. *If you have a smartphone, many phones can track your screen time and the apps that you're using the most. Check it out. You might be really surprised by how much time you're spending on certain apps.*

2. *Set yourself out a plan or a schedule. You may want to spend one hour at the gym today. So, pencil that into your day. Try to see where or if you can move things around.*

3. *Plan out your week. If you don't have much to do on Monday, but you know you have a project due that Friday, work on the project. It is five days early, but you are sure to get some work done. Something may come up during the week that prevents you from getting any more work done.*

4. *Don't procrastinate. We know, this one is a tough one. But if you don't procrastinate you won't dread it and it won't cause you as much stress.*

5. *Set limits. You can set digital limits on social media and game apps. You can do this through the settings on your phone, TV, computer, iPad, and more.*

6. *If you're always late in the morning, create a playlist of songs that equals exactly thirty minutes (or however long you want it to be). Start it when your alarm goes off. That way you know how long it's been when you hear certain songs in the playlist after a while. When the music ends, you know it'll be time to leave.*

7. *Delegate. If there are things that other people can do for you, have them do it. This will leave you more time for the things only you can do.*

8. *Wake up earlier. You can set your alarm for an extra thirty minutes earlier than you normally do. This will give you extra time throughout your day.*

9. *Organize. If you spend an hour a day every morning looking for your work stuff, you may need to get it ready the night before. Organizing your stuff can also make it easier to find things. This saves you time from looking for something later.*

10. *Deal with your stress. Being stressed out can keep your mind preoccupied. You may be too focused on what else is happening, or will happen, instead of what's currently happening or what you need to get done. Stress can distract you from what you need to get done.*

Many times, you can't get things done because you say you don't have enough time. There are times, however, that you're just not dividing your time up wisely. You can divide your time into ways that make you the most efficient.

Now, how do you decide what gets most of your time? You need to balance you needs, wants, and priorities. Your needs include things like work (sometimes), family, personal health, etc. Wants include going shopping, playing on your phone, or going out for fun. You will arrange your time slots based on what means the most to you and what requires the most time.

You need to be realistic about your time demands. You can't leave out important parts like commuting and waiting. You must include the time to get to different places. At first, you need to be patient and flexible with yourself. You're going to be making changes so it's something to get used to.

If you're used to playing on your phone for an hour before bed, don't try and say you won't do it at all. You could be setting yourself up for failure. Instead, play for thirty minutes then go to sleep. Eventually you may be able to get that down completely and you'll have more time for sleep.

Time management is about give and take. There are only so many minutes and hours in a day. You can't make new time, but you can make the best of the time you have. To do this, you have to decide what you're going to take time away from to give to something else.

Many times, this may not be an issue. We have things that we can easily slide off our schedule; that way we can do other things. However, there are times where you're stuck between a rock and a hard place. You have two things going on at once. What happens when you've overbooked?

- *Determine why you overbooked. Did you have a meeting to attend, and you offered to pick your daughter up from soccer practice? Or do you have a date tonight, but you have to finish a project by midnight?*

- *Determine which one you're needed the most at. Are you needed more at your work or your niece's ballet recital? Are you needed at your in-laws' house for dinner or catching up with a friend from out of town?*

- *Think about which event you want to go to the most. The tasks might both be bothersome, but you might like one more than the other.*

- *Can one of them be rescheduled? Maybe you can do one tonight and reschedule the other for next week.*

- *Which task will be more forgiving? Will your in-laws be more upset or your friend if you miss dinner?*

It can be easy to leave ourselves out of our daily schedule. We may think we don't need or require any time, but just a 5-minute meditation in the bathroom stall between meetings can be enough, some days, just to keep our head afloat.

You can make daily schedules, weekly, monthly, etc. A daily planner or agenda can be a critical tool for people pleasers everywhere. They can check their planner before saying yes, to make sure they're available. This agenda can also act as an excuse if someone is asking you to do something for them. You can say "Let me check my agenda. I'll get back to you if I can." This lets them know that if you can't do it, you won't reach out. This can prevent the awkward second ask in the future.

In some circumstances, you can multitask or combine two requests. You can see if you have a request that overlaps with something you're needing. For example, if you need to make a personal call but you promised your boss you would go pick up their lunch, you can make your call while getting the food or waiting on it.

It's not beneficial in all cases to multitask. Your performance goes down a lot once you are focusing on something else. If you're doing two things at once, you can confuse the two and mess them up. In the long run, it will save time to do it correctly alone the first time, rather than during a second try.

They always say, "Use your time wisely." They've never given better advice. You can do many things that can help you in many ways. One of the great ways to spend your time is learning self-love and self-confidence in therapy.

If you have a backfall and say yes a few times, you can use time management skills to make time for your tasks. This way you can get your tasks done without over-stressing yourself. Even with every free minute of your day scheduled, it can get exhausting. There are more ways you can help yourself when you just can't say no.

Therapy

Therapy can be used as a joke for some. For many, it is lifesaving. Therapy is commonly perceived as weak by society. It seems as though only people who have real trouble have to see a therapist. In reality, therapy is great for anyone. Whether they have court-ordered therapy or they're self-seeking, therapy can be used to help people in all aspects of life.

Cognitive behavioral therapy is as effective as medication in various psychological disorders. There are numerous studies that show the benefits of therapy in many areas. People need therapy for many different reasons.

Therapy can be short-term or long-term. It can last anywhere from a few visits to a few months. Therapy is different for everyone. It is all about learning about yourself and what you need to make yourself happier. It may take some a few days, while others it could take years.

Cognitive behavior therapy is a psychological treatment that can be used to treat various mental disorders. It involves focusing on unhelpful or faulty thoughts, behaviors, or thinking patterns. It also helps us unlearn these thoughts, behaviors, and thinking patterns. When we unlearn these poor patterns, therapy can help teach us to replace them with good patterns.

Therapy is beneficial for teaching us coping mechanisms for the future problems we may encounter. These coping mechanisms can be used to relieve symptoms and make our lives happier. Therapy also shows us that we have a support system. Group therapy can also be beneficial for showing a large group of support.

Cognitive behavioral therapy is beneficial for:

1. *Learning to recognize unhealthy thinking and behavior of our own. We understand what these behaviors look and sound like so we can attempt to fix or change them for our better. When we realize we are making these mistakes, we can stop.*

2. *Learning more about the motivation and behaviors of others.*

3. *Leaning how to use new problem-solving skills to cope with various difficult situations we encounter.*

4. *Creating more confidence in our own abilities.*

5. *Teaching us to face our fears rather than avoiding them.*

6. *Using role play to become prepared for possible problems in the future.*

7. *Learning how to keep yourself calm and relaxed.*

In a psychiatrist and patient relationship, they will create the treatment plan. It may contain some, none, or all of the above techniques. First, the psychiatrist and patient will determine the problem and then decide how to fix it.

During therapy you, essentially, learn to be your own therapist. You develop ideas and techniques that you can use to keep yourself in therapy for as long as you need it. Eventually, those coping mechanisms will turn into a habit, which will come naturally.

Some therapists may focus on the past to heal any previous trauma. Others may focus on the future and help you attain goals. Therapists will help you get through your current trauma and get you to move forward in your life.

Therapists will help you with getting through problems you have with yourself. Anything you might have trouble with regarding yourself, you can see a therapist to get through it.

A Thoughtful Yes

If you must say yes, make sure you think about it first. Popping off a quick yes without thinking can put you between a rock and a hard place. When someone is asking you something, take time to pause and think. The silence will make you look more powerful and confident.

When someone requests something from you, you can say something that will let them know you will reach out to them later. If you tell them, "I'll get with you," you should get back with them. Even if you are going to say no, still reach out to them. This stops them from reaching out to you again. It also shows them that you will reach out to them when you say you will. That way the next time they ask, they won't expect an answer right then.

When you do say yes, you can say yes with conditions. If they genuinely need your help, they will be open to making negotiations. For example, you could say, "I'm happy to help you but it will have to wait until next week," or "If we can be back before 5:00 p.m. then we can go." This is a compromise that is great for both the people pleaser and the person requesting.

Being thoughtful about your yes allows you to think through what you have going on and whether you actually have time to help. Even if you end up saying yes, you will have thought it through. That way you won't get the initial wave of panic that follows accepting more responsibility onto your plate.

Pausing also shows you are confident in your schedule and your abilities to handle situations. It can show you're loyal to your word and you're going to think about it before you commit to it.

A thoughtful yes is taking the time to empathize with another person. You are working to try and rearrange your schedule to accommodate them. It's helpful to make thoughtful decisions to increase your commitment to each responsibility.

During this silence, think about what you currently have going on. Do you have time? Think about what else you need to get done. Now, even if you do have time, do you have the emotional and mental capacity? It's important to make sure you're leaving time for your emotions in your schedule.

A thoughtful yes can mean you won't overbook yourself. You can remember something you have to do before you say yes. That way you won't book yourself in two places at once (as much as we would love to do that).

It will also make you feel more confident in yourself. You will feel more confident that you can get things done if you've thought about it. You also trust yourself not to say yes when you don't think you can do it.

Chapter 10: Make a Game Plan

Now that we've discussed all parts of being a people pleaser, it's time to understand how we are going to implement this book into our lives.

You've probably read a few things throughout the book that have stuck out to you and you're going to remember for your next interaction. You've probably learned some new things that are exciting and have also read some stuff that you've thought is just ridiculous.

That's the beauty of it! It's your life and you can interpret things the way you want. People pleasers can tend to be cookie cutter—cookie cutter meaning they read everything, and they believe everything they read. They pay attention to detail in case they need to recall the information later, while trying to people please.

This will be your journey. You are to take your knowledge from the book and combine it with your knowledge now to mold your life into something different. It won't be overnight. Or it might. It could be a week from now or it could be months. That's another beauty—it's your journey. So, don't get discouraged when things don't go your way. Don't get discouraged if you don't change in the next week.

You could even forget about this book for weeks. You could spiral into a depression from constantly being overwhelmed and overworked and remember this book. You can come back to it, get remotivated, and start to implement the information all over again. It may take you once, or it could take you multiple times. No matter what, it's your journey.

Now, it's important to understand how to make a game plan.

1. *First, evaluate your life. Focus on the aspects of your life that you want to change. You can make a list of areas that you'd like to work on the most. Now is your time to open up to yourself. Don't be harsh or overly critical. Don't make an attack list of yourself.*

   - *You can refer back to your moral inventory. You can also look more into your characteristics and personality. This will tell you a lot about yourself.*

2. *Second, determine how you are going to be able to change in each environment. For example, ask yourself what you can do to make your experience better. Say no to your boss when they ask? Be honest about your opinions with your family? In each situation you can make ways that you can change yourself.*

3. *Third, start to practice. Book a fake appointment and adhere to it, no matter what someone says. You need to believe that you are busy during this time. When it comes to that time, you will be able to use it any way you want. This will give you practice for when you have a real obligation and you have to say no.*

4. *Fourth, keep track of your successes. When you have this small journal of successes, you can look back at*

it when you need support. This will give you a motivational boost.

> • *You can also create rewards and incentives for yourself. If you successfully tell your boss no to an extra project, take yourself to the movies or have your favorite dinner that night. You can also set yourself up for success. If you know you're going to be put in a compromising position, set yourself an incentive. If you stick to the plan, you get something you want. It's a win-win.*

5. *Fifth, lock in your support team. Make a mental list of people who you can trust to talk with you about what you're doing. In many cases, you can find a mentor.*

> • *A mentor is someone who is a trusted advisor. You can go to them for answers, advice, information, and more. A mentor can be beneficial for showing you the ways that are the most beneficial for you. They can also talk to you enough to help you figure out what you want.*

6. *Last but not least, return back to your support system, yourself, and this book to get you through the tough times. Sometimes you relapse and you need help getting back on track. You may even want to look back and compare yourself now to what you were. Are you better? The same? Occasionally assess your progress until you're happy with all of your decisions.*

The one thing you need the most to be successful is your motivation. Our motivation acts as our passion and purpose. What are you doing this for? Who are you doing this for? The motivation statement is something we can look forward to when we're feeling down or depressed.

You can also create your own mission statement. A mission statement is not just a powerful message, but also a goal that people are aiming for. A mission statement is stated as if it is already in effect. For example, a people pleasers' mission statement could be, "To be a helpful, but self-aware coworker, who spends equal time between work and family." You can create your own mission statement to suit your personal needs.

Implementing Change Within

Throughout our lives, we pick ourselves apart. We find things that we don't like and want to change. We find things that we wish were different. As we grow, these things may change. But our desire to be bigger and better is always there.

There are many ways you can improve yourself and change yourself from who you are to who you want to be. This type of reinvention invades our life every so often. We may experience someone or something that makes us realize that we want to be different.

Anytime we feel like we need a reinvention, we feel like we need to make progress. We see this change as a form of growth, and every living thing is constantly growing, whether that be physically, emotionally, mentally, or spiritually.

Personal growth is a journey. You can't make a few changes and be "done." It isn't a destination. Seeking personal growth will allow you a continuous flow of opportunities. With these new opportunities you can keep learning new things about yourself.

- *Look at yourself outside of yourself. Just as with a sculptor and clay, see yourself as a mound of endless possibilities.*

- *Don't forget to focus on the habits that caused the change you want to make. Focus on the habits that make you a people pleaser. Change those habits with the current behavior.*

- *No matter what happens, you have to practice. It will get easier over time. Then eventually it won't require any effort at all. It takes a conscious effort.*

- *Set goals that you will be able to reach. You won't be able to wake up and say, "You know what? I'm not going to be impatient anymore." You will set yourself up for success when you understand that your bad habits won't be solved overnight. Start small and pick one event.*

  - *Say you are going to be more patient for your morning commute. We can all be in a rush and traffic can be infuriating. Make it a promise to be patient every time you drive. Once you've practiced and mastered one thing, you can move onto another situation or event.*

- *Make sure you are holding yourself accountable. If you don't ask yourself the hard questions, then you won't truly work toward what you want because you're avoiding yourself. Many of us can get in our own way when we're trying to change.*

- *Keep others in your life who will hold you accountable. Being told yes all of the time may show that they're just telling you what they think you want to hear. Keep people in your life who are going to be honest with you. That way you can use this tough feedback that's essential for personal growth.*

- *You have to take risks for personal change and growth. This is when you say no and you're not sure of the outcomes. The risks will show you what you're capable of, boost your confidence, and keep you motivated to push through your journey.*

If you're unsure whether you should say yes or no, give yourself a mental map to use when you need help with decision-making. You can remember this diagram the next time you're in a situation and you need help.

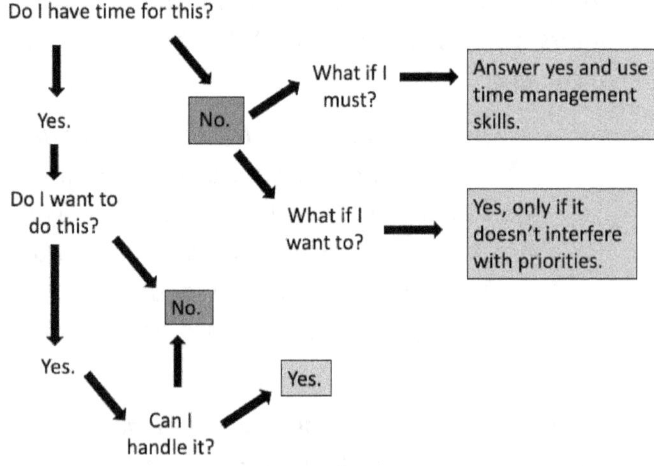

Steps to a Happier Life

Life is different for everyone. It's all about how we perceive our lives. You are the main character of your life. You make decisions about yourself and go through your daily routines. You may be thinking it's a massive and intimidating responsibility to change your life. Some people make the plans but don't commit. Instead of concentrating on the large steps, you can use little steps to reach your large goal though a series of small goals.

You see, we all have little flaws that we aren't aware of. These parts of us can make us nervous, as well as our surroundings. We have more control over our lives than we sometimes think we do. There are everyday tasks that you can do to make yourself a happier person.

<u>First, always stay positive.</u> Think of things in a positive light. Did your boss say they had no faith in you? This is a great chance to prove them wrong. Did you find out your staff was talking bad about you? This is a chance to resolve any problems that could be slowing down productivity. When we know about these problems, we can work to change them.

When we get these bad thoughts, they are brought on and controlled by our feelings. You know how when it's raining, we all want to stay in bed? It's like that. Unfortunately, negativity can be found all around us. We can't control this, but what we can control is our *reaction* to this.

Our reaction can completely change the outcome of the action. If you view the situation in a positive light, you won't get so negative and frustrated with yourself. You'll understand that this is merely an opportunity, rather than a challenge. Plus, this feels so much better than thinking you've failed. Tell yourself what you learned, instead of dwelling on how you failed.

People are afraid of failure. They avoid certain thoughts and situations because they're afraid of what could happen. Failure is a wonderful opportunity to learn what *not* to do. You now understand that it can't be done that way, and you can use your results to try again and get better and better. So, when you fail, stay positive: this is only an opportunity to get better.

You can use positive affirmations when you're trying to stay positive. They can be used to remind you of success you're having in other areas of your life. It can also give you motivation to work harder in other areas of your life.

Surround yourself with positive people. Emotions are contagious and having people around you who are positive will make it easier to be positive. They will also feed off your positivity, so it'll be a circle of positivity.

Don't focus on the negative thoughts. They can overtake our brain and prevent us from getting back to the positive thoughts. It can throw off our mood for the rest of the day. If we do get back into a good mood, we will have had to expend mental energy while being negative.

Staying active helps with overthinking and overanalyzing. Being still and alone can cause you to get lost in your head. Not only will exercise make you feel better, but it'll also make it easier to be positive.

<u>Second, set your alarm earlier.</u> Even if it's thirty minutes. You can take advantage of this time in many ways. You can get to work earlier and get a good parking spot. You can meditate in your bedroom before getting up. You can shower and take your time on your makeup.

Successful individuals are known for waking up early. They understand this time is important for strategic thinking, planning, and getting organized. This can also be some well-deserved "me" time. That way you start your day with a positive outlook and a calm mind.

Keep track of time as you're getting up and moving in the morning. It can throw off your entire mood and day if you have to rush out the door in the morning.

<u>Third, clean up after yourself as soon as you are done.</u> If you're eating lunch at your desk, clean it up and throw away any trash before going back to work. The litter can distract you if you don't get it picked up.

When waking up in the morning, make your bed. This starts your day with discipline and gets you motivated to complete your day. This minor chore can make you feel accomplished before you even leave the house. It may sound silly, but people who make their beds in the morning are happier, more successful, and invoke a sense of control.

When you have breakfast, you could use a bowl and a coffee cup. It may seem quicker to throw it in the sink and run out the door. But set your alarm just a few minutes earlier in time to clean up after yourself. If you don't, these daily dishes could pile up into a sink that bothers you for days. Especially if you don't have time or energy to do them later in the day.

<u>Fourth, don't be predictable.</u> When we do the same thing day in and day out, it puts us in a boring routine. Once a week, look to break out of your comfort zone. If there's something you've been wanting to do, try to make time to get it done.

Creating our own new experiences allows us to gain new perspectives and opportunities. It boosts our energy and makes it easier for us to change. The more we experience, the more we know what we like and don't like about ourselves.

With new experiences, you can find more habits and coping mechanisms you can use in your everyday life during change. You can pick 2 – 3 different activities and do them randomly throughout the week. That way you can decide what you feel like doing for that day.

    <u>Fifth, stay optimistic.</u> Understand that failure is part of being a human and despite failure, you are still a great human. Your failures don't define you, but merely how you react to them defines you. Be grateful for the things that happened to you that day, rather than everything that went badly.

    Try not to complain. This doesn't mean don't vent. It's important to express your emotions to others, especially if it's stress or annoyance. Otherwise, we could blow up and say and do things we can't take back.

    One of the best ways to stay optimistic is to have a daily gratitude journal. Studies have found that having a gratitude journal can have benefits for both physical and mental health.

- *People who have a gratitude journal are more likely to have fewer physical symptoms, be more optimistic about our futures, and exercise more.*

- *Keeping a daily gratitude journal can improve and increase enthusiasm, determination, alertness, energy, attentiveness, and duration of sleep.*

- *Having a gratitude journal can improve signs of anxiety and depression.*

- *These people are more likely to offer help or emotional support to others.*
  - *They also place less of a value on materialistic items.*

- *Practicing daily gratitude can even lower the chances of coronary artery disease.*

Sincerely thanking people for being a part of your life and helping you can make them happy, as well as yourself.

<u>Lastly, don't compare yourselves to others.</u> This is one of the best ways to set yourself up for failure. Everyone has completely different lives, so you can't expect to look, sound, or feel exactly like someone else.

There is always someone who is going to "look better," make more money, seem more productive, have themselves better put together, etc. Some friends and family may be retired, others could be just starting a career. Regardless, everyone is in different areas of their lives.

Comparing yourself to others makes you unhappily preoccupied with what others think of you. You spend more time on what you mean to others instead of what you mean to yourself. You'll be miserable, constantly trying to catch up with someone else.

Therapy

Therapy provides a safe place for us to explore our past. We can uncover any trauma or issues we may have had in the past. Our past trauma can cause emotional damage. This damage leads to unhealthy conditions, thoughts, actions, and behaviors.

There's a negative stigma surrounding therapy. People think that therapy is only for weak people or those who have mental illness, but therapy can be beneficial for everyone. Therapy acts as a tool for you to use to better your mental health condition.

<u>Benefits of Therapy</u>

1. *Therapy can be beneficial in the short term and long term. The positive effects from therapy can last a lifetime. Therapy provides you with tools that you can use to cope during hard times in the future, even if you're not currently in therapy. The more you use these techniques throughout your life, the stronger they're going to get. This can be considered self-therapy.*

2. *When you undergo therapy, your physical symptoms also get treated. Because poor mental conditions are linked to pain and physical ailments, when you treat the mental conditions you ultimately treat the physical conditions related. Bodies can react to stress and mental pain through sleeping problems, headaches, stomach aches, and digestive issues.*

3. *When you avoid talking about trauma and pain, you bottle up your emotions. After so long of being bottled up you're going to explode. Therapy can avoid these large blowups by allowing you to work through your emotions without swallowing them down. When you don't properly express your emotions, it can lead to negative thought patterns that affect all parts of your life.*

4. *Therapy helps you find internal and misplaced anger. Many times when you have suppressed anger, it can come out as passive-aggressive behavior. It can also lead to negative moods and inability to handle simple situations. This anger that we hold inside can also taint our view of those*

around us. It can create these negative thoughts and ideas based on what we think others are doing.

5. *Therapy can help you work through your own problems, but it can also teach you about the problems of others. When you learn to understand your own emotions, you can better understand the emotions of others.*

6. *We are always going to experience problems, whether they're big or small. There is a chance of relapse back into your own thoughts or ways after graduating out of therapy. When we encounter problems that may send us back to where we were, therapy can help teach us what to do for future problems. Once you've had therapy, you know what you can do to improve your outcomes after these problems. Therapy will teach you how to avoid being absorbed by problems so you can focus on how to solve them.*

7. *When you're constantly obsessing over problems in your head, they can just feel like huge clouds of smoke. You can't see the beginning or end. When you talk (or write) about your feelings, you're making it clear in your head. You can create the problem into a shape: beginning and end. This way you can clarify your thinking.*

8. *Therapy can be a reminder that you're not alone in your feelings. It is proof that others are struggling as bad as, if not worse than, you. Therapy can also introduce you to others that can be experiencing the same things you are. For example, you can join a support group or partake in group therapy.*

9. *Therapy can bring about changes in your brain. When we make certain decisions and partake in certain actions and behaviors, our brains release chemicals. These chemicals can change the emotions we have associated with specific events or phrases. Therapy can activate the medial prefrontal cortex, the amygdala, the hippocampus, and the anterior cingulate cortex. These parts of the brain are responsible for information processing and decision making.*

10. *Cognitive behavioral therapy can show you the negative thought patterns that you tend to partake in. It can teach you how to recognize these patterns and avoid further damage. Therapy leads to more positive mental habits, which decreases the symptoms of anxiety and depression.*

11. *Therapy can help you with self-medicating. We may use various unhealthy coping mechanisms to get through our troubles now. It can be drugs, alcohol, cigarettes, isolation, and much more. These behaviors can become addicting and make your mental conditions worse.*

12. *Attending therapy can show the next generation that therapy is for everyone, not just those who are mentally ill. By dealing with your own problems, you allow others to see you as an example. You leave more positivity in your path and can even teach others some of what you learned in therapy. You can be there for someone who needs help, and you could even end up saving someone's life.*

When you meet with a therapist or psychologist, you are showing an interest in improving your life. You acknowledge the benefits of pursuing therapy and you know you could improve your performance by attending.

About one in five adult Americans has a mental health condition. Mental conditions vary with every person, even if they have the same diagnosis. What anxiety looks like for a 22-year-old college student will look different than a 35-year-old man looking for a promotion. These conditions can range from mild to severe.

In severe cases, some people may need therapy for their people-pleasing behaviors. Therapy is nothing to be ashamed of and everyone can benefit from therapy at some point in their lives. Many conditions may lead to people-pleasing behaviors. It's important to recognize if you have more symptoms; you may need to see a doctor for further testing.

Depression

Depression is referred to as clinical depression or major depressive disorder. This is a serious but common mood disorder. A mood disorder is the inability of the mind and body to regulate emotions properly. These symptoms can affect your feelings, daily activities, thinking, eating, working, sleeping, and every other aspect of your life.

Depression isn't to be confused with a few bad days. It can be short-term, such as after the death of a loved one. It could be long-term as well, which may indicate that there is a chemical imbalance in the brain. Depression is considered a problem if it persists for longer than two weeks.

There are different types of depression that happen for different reasons. They also last different amounts of time.

- ***Persistent depressive disorder*** *(dysthymia) is having depressive symptoms for longer than two years. The symptoms may range from mild to severe but must be overall present for more than two years to be considered persistent depressive disorder.*

- ***Postpartum depression*** *is experienced by women after childbirth. This is not to be confused with the "baby blues." This is a common form of depression that will usually resolve within two weeks after birth. Full-blown major depression can be experienced by women after delivery, or even during pregnancy. Symptoms include anxiety, exhaustion, and extreme sadness.*

- ***Seasonal affective disorder*** *is when depression gets worse during the winter months. This is largely because there is less sunlight. This type of depression tends to get better in the spring and summer. Social withdrawal, increased sleep, winter depression, and weight gain accompanies seasonal affective disorder.*

- ***Psychotic depression*** *shows when a person is having severe depression and a form of psychosis. This includes disturbing thoughts based on false beliefs, like delusions and hallucinations. Depressive symptoms show through hallucinations of illness, guilt, and poverty.*

- ***Bipolar disorder*** *is similar to depression, but different in the fact that it is emotional extremes. When you're bipolar, you experience levels of high energy and mania followed by low-level moods (depression).*

Some of the symptoms and signs of depression include:

- *Irritability*
- *Suicidal thoughts or attempts*
- *Aches and pains, cramps, headaches, and digestive problems without clear cause or cannot be helped with treatment*
- *Difficulty remembering, making decisions, or concentrating*
- *Early-morning awakening, oversleeping, or difficulty sleeping*
- *Having trouble with being still or feelings of restlessness*
- *Fatigue and decreased energy*
- *Loss of interest in daily activities and hobbies*
- *Feelings of pessimism or hopelessness*
- *Persistent anxious, "empty," or sad moods*
- *Talking or moving slowly*
- *Weight and/or appetite changes*

Symptoms are different for everyone. Some may experience more than one or all of these symptoms, while others may only experience a few. Symptoms can be eased, and made worse, by various situations. More than one symptom for an increased period of time is required to get a diagnosis.

Depression can cause people-pleasing behaviors as an attempt to gain the approval and acceptance of others. People pleasers think that if they say yes to everyone, they will be happy and included in others' activities. They place their happiness in the hands of others. Depression can cause people to do whatever they need to do to feel happy again.

Even the most severe cases of depression can be treated. Psychotherapy and medication are the top two treatments for depression. Short-term depression may be treated with short-term treatment. Some individuals may be able to stop treatment once symptoms improve. Others may need treatment for the entirety of their lives. Either way, it's always important to speak with a physician before starting or stopping medication for depression.

<u>Anxiety</u>

We all have common stressors. A new job. First day at a new school. Going on a date. These "butterflies" in your stomach remind you that you're nervous and excited about what could happen next. This is healthy anxiety.

When you have crippling fear, it's hard to live your daily life. When nervousness becomes constant fear, then you're showing signs of an anxiety disorder. An anxiety disorder is shown when you cannot control your nervousness, it leads to panic attacks, or it keeps you from living your daily life.

There is not any one certain test that can be done to diagnose anxiety. Rather, the diagnosis process includes various tests, examinations, and questionnaires to come to a conclusion.

There may be underlying conditions that can cause anxiety. Digestive issues, chronic pain and conditions, hormone imbalances, and more. Just because you are experiencing symptoms of anxiety doesn't mean you have anxiety disorder. You may just be experiencing an increased time of stress.

Working hard for a promotion, lack of or inconsistent sleep, exhaustion, and poor diet can all lead to anxiety. However, this type of anxiety can be fixed with a few lifestyle changes. Eating more fruits and vegetables, getting more sleep, or finally finishing that project will take away the nervousness you may be experiencing.

However, long-term nervousness may need medication and/or therapy to help. There is no definite cure for anxiety, and it must be managed in different ways or it can become debilitating. Some people experience anxiety so severe that they can't enter an elevator, start a relationship, or sometimes even leave their home.

Symptoms of anxiety include:

- *Dry mouth*
- *Worry and apprehension*
- *Restlessness*
- *Tingling or numbness*
- *Fear*
- *Distress*
- *Shortness of breath*
- *Feeling dizzy or faint*
- *Sweating*
- *Hot flashes or chills*

Symptoms are different for everyone. They may range from mild to severe and short-term or long-term. Anxiety disorder may also cause anxiety attacks and panic attacks. An anxiety attack can come on gradually. It may not be triggered by anything specifically and is different for everyone. Two different people with different symptoms can each claim to have anxiety attacks.

Panic attacks, however, can either be triggered or not. There may be external factors that cause a panic attack, or they can be unexpected without obvious cause. External triggers can be caused by situations that give you severe anxiety. Anxiety attacks, and even panic attacks, can happen to anyone. However, if you have had more than one, then you might need to be diagnosed, as this can be a sign of panic disorder.

When you feel a panic or anxiety attack about to begin, you can:

- *Take deep, slow breaths. If you feel out of control of your breath, focus on each exhale and inhale. Focus on air going into your stomach. This can allow your shoulders to relax. When you exhale, count to four. Keep doing this until your breath slows down.*

- *Recognize that you're having an anxiety or panic attack. Understand that you know these symptoms and they're going to stop after some time.*

- *Mindfulness is a great way to pull yourself back into reality. You can focus on other parts of reality to grab yourself. You can focus on what you see, what you smell, what you hear, and what you can touch. You can describe how something feels.*

- *Relaxation techniques can be beneficial for keeping you calm during a time of anxiety. Using lavender as aromatherapy, taking a bath, closing your eyes, and focusing on muscle relaxation can improve relaxation.*

Treatment for anxiety includes a number of options. First, medication can be used to improve symptoms from anxiety. These medications can be used for short-term or long-term outcomes. Some medication may be taken every day, while others may only be taken during times of need (as needed).

Medication is different for everyone. Across multiple drugs and doses, everyone can react to the pills differently. It's important to determine the side effects of your medication before starting. This way you know what to look for and you can determine whether you need to continue on that medication or dosage.

Getting aligned with medication can take some time. You may have to cycle through a few drugs before settling on one that will work. Typically, medication for mental conditions takes about 30 days before you notice a difference in symptoms and behavior. Some medications may also make anxiety worse before making it better.

If you feel like a medication is working, but not well enough, your doctor may increase the dosage or add on another medication. Being diagnosed with anxiety at a young age can indicate that it will be a lifelong problem and can continuously get worse if not treated.

A second treatment for anxiety includes (yes, you guessed it) therapy. Therapy allows those with anxiety to discuss why they're so anxious. You can get to the root of your anxiety and try to find ways to cope with what's causing your problems.

Therapy can be found pretty easily. You can perform a simple Google search for therapists in your area. You may also be able to ask friends and family for recommendations. Meeting and talking with your primary care doctor can also lead you in the right direction.

Therapy can be paid for out of pocket or through insurance. Every insurance is different, and every therapist is different. Costs and prices will be different with everyone. It's important to understand payment when starting therapy so your medical bills don't affect the quality of your therapy.

Conclusion

Now, you can:

- *Better control your responses when being asked a favor or request.*

- *Say no and stand behind your answer.*

- *Trust in yourself and listen to your needs.*

- *Cultivate the self-confidence and independence to set boundaries and stick with them.*

- *Know more about yourself.*

Okay, now take a deep breath. It seems like this is a lot of information to take in at once, and it is. You may be feeling a number of things. You could feel motivated to go out and make these changes right now. Hang onto that feeling and go out and make those changes right now. It's best to work now while you're motivated—that way you can continue on with your path to success. However, be sure to pace yourself so you don't burn yourself out. If you start too fast, you'll run out of steam and end up giving up on your goal.

You can also be feeling overwhelmed. Overwhelmed by the information, overwhelmed by what you figured out about yourself, overwhelmed by what you're realizing others have been doing to you, etc. Do understand that this feeling is only going to last for a moment. You can understand that you're overwhelmed and practice some of the tips that we talked about in the book to handle some of the feelings you're experiencing right now.

Some of you may feel relieved. You may feel like you're not alone in what you've been feeling. You may be relieved that there are changes you can make to alter your life right now. That relief you're feeling right now shows that you've been under stress and pressure. Use this relief to build your motivation to start saying no and standing up for yourself.

This book isn't meant to make you feel scared or inadequate. This isn't "one size fits all." The beauty of the book is that you can take what you need from it. You can keep the rest of the information for when you need it, or even pass the knowledge on to others. You can refer back to the book when you need a reminder for what you're doing.

Now think to yourself what the definition of a people pleaser is. Do you think that includes you? Do you know someone who's a people pleaser? I think we can all agree that a people pleaser is someone who's willing to bend and fold for the opportunity to please others. Being a people pleaser can feel fulfilling; however, when it's done incorrectly it can seriously cause harm for you and those around you.

Overall, there are a couple of things that you're going to want to do to learn how to stop being a people pleaser. First, you're going to want to discover who you are. You can't properly help other people when you don't know yourself. When you know who you really are, you're more confident. You're going to learn how to stop being so hard on yourself, and find these unhealthy behaviors that upset you, then fix them.

Next, you're going to address any negative experiences, trauma, or insecurities that you might have.

Reach into the deep, dark parts of yourself and find out the real reason behind your thoughts and actions. You're going to work on your lack of self-esteem and your ability to be so impressionable by the people around you. You want to be the one that leaves an impression on others.

Moving forward, you'll set boundaries for yourself and your life. These boundaries are going to protect you from hurting or harming yourself. These boundaries are also going to keep those around you safe from being hurt by you. When you set boundaries, you're taking part in self-compassion. Make your boundaries and learn how to stick with them.

Next, you're going to say no. That's right. Now you can say no. Not only because you know how to say no, but you trust yourself more to say no. You've got all this knowledge and confidence so you can be certain you're going to start saying no. It may even be unconscious. Reading this book may stick in your mind and you can instinctively start saying no. For some of you this may be easier than for others. But one sure thing is that everyone can do it.

Don't forget to stay strong. At this point you've probably created some ways of how you're going to stay strong. Throughout reading you've probably paused and thought to yourself what you would do if you were in a certain situation. This is you creating coping mechanisms. When you create a plan to stay strong, make sure you include coping mechanisms. These can get you over the hard times when you can't reach out to your support team. Stay strong when handling reactions. They can go one way or the other, good or bad. Regardless of the outcome, you have to trust yourself and stick by what you say.

Always remember to express yourself. Expressing yourself is one of the biggest ways to build your confidence.

Expressing yourself is different for everyone and that's the beauty of it. Whether you're expressing yourself through social interactions or activities, be aware that you're expressing yourself. Be happy in the moment that you're allowed to be you. After all, the brain changes for the better during self-expression.

Next, be assertive. Being passive gets you taken advantage of and being aggressive gets you in trouble. Being assertive gets your point across in a confident, clear, and controlled manner. When you speak with logic and reason, people are more open to listening to you versus when you're screaming and speaking out of emotion. Be confident in what you're saying, don't leave any room for guessing, and control your tone and emotions when you're delivering your message.

Now that we're at the finish line, we make a game plan. You're going to want to make these changes that you've been thinking about throughout the entire book. Once you do these changes within, you can perform your changes on the outside. It all starts with you and taking steps to a happier life. Sometimes those steps might include therapy, and that's okay. Therapy can be helpful for anyone and can be especially helpful for a person who is a severe people pleaser.

Last but not least, don't get upset. This may not work on the first try. You may use these behaviors for a week and then resort back to your old ways. You might keep saying yes for the next six months after reading this book because you think that now is not a time in your life that you can say no. One of two things are going to happen. One, you are going to get tired of what you're going through and you blow up. It will take this hard, abrupt realization for you to make the changes that you need in your life. You may not see it now, but these changes will make you happier. If you didn't actually believe that, you wouldn't have read this book.

Two, you are going to start saying no. You're going to start practicing tomorrow. You are going to take it and run with it and make the best of it that you can. Change is a different pace for everyone; it's not a race.

Reforming yourself as a people pleaser is a journey, not a destination. This isn't saying that you're never going to say yes again without regretting it. There are going to be times when you keep saying yes because you've gotten back into the routine. But now that you know what harm it can do, you can better control when you say no. Now you can determine when you want to say no and when you need to say no.

www.ingramcontent.com/pod-product-compliance
Lightning Source LLC
Chambersburg PA
CBHW060931050726
47592CB00003B/906